POETRY FOR JUNIOR STUDENTS

WITH SUGGESTIVE STUDIES

BY

SISTER ANNA LOUISE, S.C.N.

WITH A FOREWORD BY

REVEREND RICHARD QUINLAN
DIOCESAN SUPERVISOR OF SCHOOLS
ARCHDIOCESE OF BOSTON

ST. AUGUSTINE ACADEMY PRESS
HOMER GLEN, ILLINOIS

Nihil Obstat

PATRICK J. WATERS, Ph.D.
CENSOR LIBRORUM

Imprimatur

✠ WILLIAM CARDINAL O'CONNELL
ARCHBISHOP OF BOSTON

This book was originally published in 1929 by Ginn and Company.

This facsimile edition reprinted in 2019 by St. Augustine Academy Press.

ISBN: 978-1-64051-086-9

TO

OUR LADY

SEAT OF WISDOM

PREFACE

A professor of English in one of our Catholic universities said recently, "Our students today know much about poetry, but they know little poetry!" When asked to explain this remark, he replied, "They can tell me about authors and about poems, but they cannot quote passages, and very seldom do I find in their themes an allusion to a poem."

This is a general complaint. Inquiry into the cause of this condition reveals the fact that students are not getting sufficient memory training. Our curricula are so crowded with matter essential to credits that little room is left for poetry. Then, too, we are living in an age which is not artistic, but tends rather to things practical and standardized. Finally, modern fiction, photo plays, and amusements that require no memory activity today offer many other interests more appealing to the senses.

It is refreshing, however, to note that there is in progress a real revival of interest in poetry. This is shown by the recent publication of many splendid collections of verse, some of which have been prepared especially for the young.

PREFACE

Poetry, from its very nature, makes strong appeal to childhood. It is the language of ideals, the medium of emotion, the perfection of rhythm; and idealism, emotion, and rhythm are qualities inherent in humanity from the cradle to the grave. The poet sees into the heart of things, and out of this knowledge he reveals the secrets of nature and of nature's God.

Because the child has an innate love of poetry, we should give him the very best of our literature. He may not always thoroughly appreciate the poet's words, but some of their truth and beauty will sink in and prepare his mind for a fuller understanding in later life.

With this thought in mind, I have made this selection of poetry and have added questions to many of the poems to stimulate the student's interest to the end that he may be led to judge and appraise for himself the richness and beauty of our English poetry.

SISTER ANNA LOUISE

ACKNOWLEDGMENTS

Grateful acknowledgment is made to the following authors, publishers, and editors for permission to reprint selections for which they hold the copyright:

The America Press: for "The Way of the Cross," from *In Towns and Little Towns*, by Leonard Feeney, S. J.

D. Appleton and Company: for "To the Fringed Gentian," from *The Poetical Works of William Cullen Bryant*.

Reverend Hugh Francis Blunt: for "An Old Woman's Rosary."

Dodd, Mead and Company: for "The Confessional," from *Bread and Circuses*, by Helen Parry Eden.

The Dolphin Press: for the translation, by Father Paschal Robinson, of St. Francis's "Hymn to the Sun," from *The Writings of St. Francis of Assisi*.

Doubleday, Doran & Company, Inc.: for "Song for a Little House," from *Songs for a Little House*, by Christopher Morley, copyright, 1917, George H. Doran Company; and for "Trees," from *Trees and Other Poems*, by Joyce Kilmer, copyright, 1914, George H. Doran Company, publishers.

Denis A. McCarthy: for "The Green o' the Spring," from *Voices from Erin and Other Poems*.

Harcourt, Brace and Company, Inc.: for "Da Leetla Boy," from *Carmina*, by T. A. Daly. Reprinted by permission of Harcourt, Brace and Company, Inc., holders of the copyright; and for "The Toys," from *Poems*, by Coventry Patmore. Reprinted by permission of Harcourt, Brace and Company, Inc., holders of the copyright.

Henry Holt and Company: for "The Irish," from Francis Carlin's *My Ireland*. By permission of Henry Holt and Company, publishers.

ACKNOWLEDGMENTS

Houghton Mifflin Company: for "The Day is Done" and "The Builders," by Henry Wadsworth Longfellow; for extracts from "The Vision of Sir Launfal," by James Russell Lowell; for "The Rhodora," by Ralph Waldo Emerson. By permission of and by arrangement with Houghton Mifflin Company.

Blanche Mary Kelly: for "The Housewife's Prayer."

P. J. Kenedy & Sons: for "A Child's Wish," from *Poems* by Abram J. Ryan.

Francis A. Litz: for "A Bunch of Roses," "Father Damien," and "Out of Bounds" from *The Poetry of Father Tabb*.

Louis Loveman, and J. B. Lippincott Company: for "The Rain Song," by Robert Loveman.

Robert M. McBride & Co.: for "Courtesy," from *Sonnets and Verse*, by Hilaire Belloc.

G. P. Putnam's Sons: for "In Flanders Fields," from *In Flanders Fields*, by John D. McCrae. Courtesy of G. P. Putnam's Sons, publishers.

Charles Scribner's Sons: for "The Swing," from *A Child's Garden of Verses*, by Robert Louis Stevenson; for "A Ballad of Trees and the Master," from *Poems of Sidney Lanier*; for "Four Things," from *The Poems of Henry van Dyke*; for "Wynken, Blynken, and Nod" and "Little Boy Blue," from *Lullaby Land* and *Songs of Childhood*, by Eugene Field; for "The Shepherdess," from *The Poems of Alice Meynell*; for "Little Jesus," from *The Poems of Francis Thompson*.

Katharine Tynan (Mrs. Hinkson): for "The Man of the House."

CONTENTS

		PAGE
LITTLE JESUS — *EX ORE INFANTIUM*	Francis Thompson	1
TREES	Joyce Kilmer	4
THE COIN	Sara Teasdale	5
FOUR THINGS	Henry van Dyke	6
TWO WENT UP TO THE TEMPLE TO PRAY	Richard Crashaw	7
"I WANDERED LONELY AS A CLOUD"	William Wordsworth	8
A GREEN CORNFIELD	Christina Georgina Rossetti	11
TO DAFFODILS	Robert Herrick	12
THE BUILDERS	Henry Wadsworth Longfellow	15
WYNKEN, BLYNKEN, AND NOD	Eugene Field	17
THE GLOVE AND THE LIONS	Leigh Hunt	20
BEFORE SLEEPING		22
THE LAMB	William Blake	23
THE TIGER	William Blake	24
A CHILD'S THOUGHT OF GOD	Elizabeth Barrett Browning	26
SONG FOR A LITTLE HOUSE	Christopher Morley	27
THE TOYS	Coventry Patmore	29
SEVEN TIMES ONE	Jean Ingelow	31
EPITAPH	Samuel Taylor Coleridge	33
A BALLAD OF TREES AND THE MASTER	Sidney Lanier	34
I SEE HIS BLOOD UPON THE ROSE	Joseph Mary Plunkett	36
IN THE FIELDS		37
THE IRISH	Francis Carlin	38
THE SWING	Robert Louis Stevenson	40
"TIME, YOU OLD GIPSY MAN"	Ralph Hodgson	41
TO THE FRINGED GENTIAN	William Cullen Bryant	45
THE GREEN O' THE SPRING	Denis A. McCarthy	47

CONTENTS

		PAGE
THE MAN OF THE HOUSE	Katharine Tynan	49
MARY IMMACULATE	Eleanor C. Donnelly	52
FOR THOSE WHO FAIL	Joaquin Miller	53
"WHAT IS IN HEAVEN?"	Richard Rolle	54
THE MAGNIFICAT	St. Luke's Gospel	56
AN OLD CHRISTMAS CAROL		58
A CHILD'S WISH	Abram J. Ryan	59
AN OLD WOMAN'S ROSARY	Hugh F. Blunt	61
THE DAY IS DONE	Henry Wadsworth Longfellow	63
SWEET AND LOW	Alfred Tennyson	66
I WALKED A MILE	John B. Tabb	67
THE QUALITY OF MERCY	William Shakespeare	68
COURTESY	Hilaire Belloc	70
CHARITY	Robert Burns	72
ABOU BEN ADHEM	Leigh Hunt	73
JUSTICE	William Shakespeare	74
THE CONFESSIONAL	Helen Parry Eden	75
OUT OF BOUNDS	John B. Tabb	77
THE WAY OF THE CROSS	Leonard Feeney, S. J.	78
JUBILATE DEO	Psalm 99	79
TO-DAY	Thomas Carlyle	80
FATHER DAMIEN	John B. Tabb	82
A BUNCH OF ROSES	John B. Tabb	83
THE TAX-GATHERER	John B. Tabb	83
IN FLANDERS FIELDS	John D. McCrae	84
HOHENLINDEN	Thomas Campbell	86
THE RHODORA	Ralph Waldo Emerson	88
THE BURIAL OF SIR JOHN MOORE	Charles Wolfe	89
SONG OF THE ANGEL	John Henry Newman	91
AVE MARIA BELLS	Charles Warren Stoddard	93
THE SHEPHERDESS	Alice Meynell	94
THE HOUSEWIFE'S PRAYER	Blanche Mary Kelly	96

CONTENTS

		PAGE
LITTLE BOY BLUE	Eugene Field	97
DA LEETLA BOY	Thomas Augustine Daly	99
"BREAK, BREAK, BREAK"	Alfred Tennyson	101
ANNABEL LEE	Edgar Allan Poe	102
"HARK, HARK! THE LARK"	William Shakespeare	105
GOD'S PRESENCE IN NATURE	Thomas Moore	106
"BLOW, BLOW"	William Shakespeare	108
SEA FEVER	John Masefield	109
"HE PRAYETH BEST"	Samuel Taylor Coleridge	112
ON THE LOSS OF THE *ROYAL GEORGE*	William Cowper	113
THE VIRGIN	William Wordsworth	115
HYMN TO THE VIRGIN	Sir Walter Scott	116
APOSTROPHE TO THE OCEAN	Lord Byron	118
THE SEA	Barry Cornwall	119
"MY HEART LEAPS UP WHEN I BEHOLD"	William Wordsworth	121
"THE YEAR'S AT THE SPRING"	Robert Browning	122
ON HIS BLINDNESS	John Milton	123
"HOW SLEEP THE BRAVE"	William Collins	125
THE RAIN SONG	Robert Loveman	126
LOCHINVAR	Sir Walter Scott	128
HYMN TO THE SUN	St. Francis of Assisi	131
HYMN	St. Francis Xavier	134
THE VISION OF SIR LAUNFAL (Prelude to Part First)	James Russell Lowell	136
THE VISION OF SIR LAUNFAL (Prelude to Part Second)	James Russell Lowell	138
ODE TO A NIGHTINGALE	John Keats	140
RUTH	Thomas Hood	142
BIOGRAPHICAL INDEX		143
INDEX OF AUTHORS		153

FOREWORD

Poetry has ever been the expression of the inmost human emotions and the noblest spiritual ideals. It will always be an inexhaustible source of thought, culture, and inspiration. The beautiful soul-stirring sentiments of such poets as Shakespeare, Tennyson, and Thompson will ever move countless souls to the contemplation of truths noble and divine. The human soul seeks its true dwelling place in the world of idealism. It cannot be confined to things earthly and material. It craves completeness of life in the nobler and spiritual realities which find their fullest expression in the poetic word. True and complete education must nourish this innate craving of the human soul. Noble and inspiring poetry admirably supplies the soul's æsthetic need for fullness and completeness of spiritual life.

Poetry is the handmaid at once of religion and of patriotism. Holy Mother Church generously and wisely makes use of spiritual canticles to stimulate devotion and inculcate ideals in the souls of her children. The Psalms of David, the Benedictus of Zachary, and the Magnificat of Mary ever Virgin have from the beginning been an integral part of the Church's beautiful liturgy. Who would attempt to measure the influence of poetry in the history of men and of nations? Every nation has its national anthem. In peace and in war the ideals of men and of nations have been largely formed and sustained in noble and thrilling poems.

In this volume the author gives in printed form the fruits of many years' successful experience in teaching poetry to children. She has carefully selected beautiful poems which stimulate cultural aspiration, patriotic devotion, and spiritual inspiration. Eminently practical suggestions are appended to enable boys and girls to comprehend the beauty of expression and the nobility of sentiment found in this epitome of poetic literature.

To teach boys and girls to love poetry is the purpose of "Poetry for Junior Students." This work represents a distinct and notable contribution to the textbook literature designed to aid teachers in the delightful task of training children in the upper grades to appreciate the beauty, worth, and power of poetic expression.

RICHARD J. QUINLAN
DIOCESAN SUPERVISOR OF SCHOOLS
ARCHDIOCESE OF BOSTON

POETRY FOR JUNIOR STUDENTS

LITTLE JESUS

Francis Thompson

Ex ore infantium, Deus, et lactentium perfecisti laudem

Little Jesus, wast Thou shy
Once, and just so small as I?
And what did it feel like to be
Out of Heaven, and just like me?
Didst Thou sometimes think of *there*,
And ask where all the angels were?
I should think that I would cry
For my house all made of sky;
I would look about the air,
And wonder where my angels were;

And at waking 'twould distress me —
Not an angel there to dress me!
Hadst Thou ever any toys,
Like us little girls and boys?
And didst Thou play in Heaven with all
The angels that were not too tall,

With stars for marbles? Did the things
Play *Can you see me?* through their wings?
And did Thy Mother let Thee spoil
Thy robes, with playing on our soil?
How nice to have them always new
In Heaven, because 'twas quite clean blue!

Didst Thou kneel at night to pray
And didst Thou join Thy hands, this way?
And did they tire sometimes, being young,
And make the prayer seem very long?
And dost Thou like it best, that we
Should join our hands to pray to Thee?
I used to think, before I knew,
The prayer not said unless we do.
And did Thy Mother at the night
Kiss Thee, and fold the clothes in right?
And didst Thou feel quite good in bed,
Kissed, and sweet, and Thy prayers said?

Thou canst not have forgotten all
That it feels like to be small:
And Thou know'st I cannot pray
To Thee in my father's way —
When Thou wast so little, say,
Couldst Thou talk Thy Father's way? —

LITTLE JESUS

So, a little Child, come down
And hear a child's tongue like Thy own;
Take me by the hand and walk,
And listen to my baby-talk.
To Thy Father show my prayer
(He will look, Thou art so fair),
And say: "O Father, I, Thy Son,
Bring the prayer of a little one."

And He will smile, that children's tongue
Has not changed since Thou wast young!

No more beautiful child's prayer has been written than this of Francis Thompson's. It is so simple and direct that it needs no explanation, other than our Lord's own words: "Out of the mouths of infants and of sucklings thou hast perfected praise." (St. Matthew xxi, 16. Psalm viii, 3.)

At what age is a child particularly shy?
At what age is he most likely to cry for things?
At what age is he most full of wonder?
At what age does a child usually wish to dress himself?
Is not the idea of "stars for marbles" a striking one?
What else have the stars been called?
What did Longfellow in "Evangeline" call them?
Do you not remember the time when you thought your prayers "not said" unless your hands were joined?
Is not the practice of joining hands an aid to prayer?

The last long stanza of the poem gives us a model of perfect prayer made to the Heavenly Father and offered through His Divine Son. What did our Lord promise to petitions made in His name?

What terrible threat has He made to those who do not become like little children?

[POEM FOR CLASS DISCUSSION]

TREES

Joyce Kilmer

I think that I shall never see
A poem lovely as a tree.

A tree whose hungry mouth is prest
Against the earth's sweet flowing breast;

A tree that looks at God all day,
And lifts her leafy arms to pray;

A tree that may in Summer wear
A nest of robins in her hair;

Upon whose bosom snow has lain;
Who intimately lives with rain.

Poems are made by fools like me,
But only God can make a tree.

THE COIN[1]

SARA TEASDALE

Into my heart's treasury
   I slipped a coin
That time cannot take,
   Nor a thief purloin.

O better than the minting
   Of a gold-crowned king
Is the safe-kept memory
   Of a lovely thing.

◇ ◇ ◇

Read this poem carefully to find out what is meant by "the coin." For what are coins used?

Does time usually take away our coins? How does it do so?

What is the meaning of "purloin"? Make that word your own by using it in a sentence.

What is the "heart's treasury"?

What sort of treasure does Holy Scripture tell us to accumulate? Give the quotation in full from St. Matthew's Gospel, Chapter VI.

[1] Reprinted from Sara Teasdale's *Flame and Shadow*. By permission of The Macmillan Company, publishers.

What is the meaning of "minting"? Father Faber has a chapter in his beautiful book *All for Jesus*, entitled "Minting Money" (for Heaven). What do you think he means by this? Designating the value of sacrifices by coins, name some of the ways in which you may mint money for our Blessed Lord.

Does the phrase "gold-crowned" add anything to your picture of a king? Why?

Notice the phrase "safe-kept" in reference to memory. Is it not expressive?

Do you not remember from your Bible history a story that ends: "But Mary kept all these words, pondering them in her heart"? Is not this a beautiful example of "the safe-kept memory of a lovely thing"?

Every poem that you will study in this book is a "lovely thing" and it was put here for you to study and ponder and commit to memory that in the end you may have a whole treasure house of "safe-kept lovely things."

[POEMS FOR CLASS DISCUSSION]

FOUR THINGS

HENRY VAN DYKE

Four things a man must learn to do
If he would make his record true:
To think without confusion clearly;
To love his fellow men sincerely;
To act from honest motives purely;
To trust in God and Heaven securely.

TWO WENT UP TO THE TEMPLE TO PRAY
Richard Crashaw

Two went to pray? Oh, rather say
One went to brag, the other to pray;

One stands up close and treads on high
Where the other dares not lend his eye;

One nearer to God's altar trod,
The other to the altar's God.

"I WANDERED LONELY AS A CLOUD"

William Wordsworth

I wandered lonely as a cloud
That floats on high o'er vales and hills,
When all at once I saw a crowd,
A host, of golden daffodils;
Beside the lake, beneath the trees,
Fluttering and dancing in the breeze.

Continuous as the stars that shine
And twinkle on the milky way,
They stretched in never-ending line
Along the margin of a bay:
Ten thousand saw I at a glance,
Tossing their heads in sprightly dance.

The waves beside them danced; but they
Out-did the sparkling waves in glee:
A poet could not but be gay,
In such a jocund company:
I gazed — and gazed — but little thought
What wealth the show to me had brought:

"I WANDERED LONELY AS A CLOUD"

For oft, when on my couch I lie
In vacant or in pensive mood,
They flash upon that inward eye
Which is the bliss of solitude;
And then my heart with pleasure fills,
And dances with the daffodils.

Read the entire poem,
In what mood was the author at the beginning of the poem? Did his mood change? How? What various emotions can you classify in the course of the poem? Do you share his feelings when you read the poem?

Will you not always think of these lines of Wordsworth when you see a "host" of daffodils?

What season of the year is depicted?

What is the arrangement of lines, and the order of rhyme? Do you like this kind of verse? See if you can find the name given to this arrangement of lines.

Do the first two lines express intensity of loneliness? What have you observed of clouds in general?

What do you think of the use of the words "crowd" and "host" applied to blossoms? What other words could have been used? Do you like those as well as the words used by Wordsworth? Why? Note the contrast between "lonely" and "crowd."

Could there be a more attractive picture than that so clearly portrayed in the lines:

> "A host of golden daffodils;
> Beside the lake, beneath the trees,
> Fluttering and dancing in the breeze."

Have you not often seen these joyous spring flowers?
Could they be other than "spring flowers" with such sprightly, buoyant airs?

See how many poems you can find containing reference to daffodils and compare them with this poem.

The second stanza estimates the number of this "crowd of daffodils." How many are there? Which line gives the greatest number? The last line emphasizes the mood of the poet. What particular word? Is that word often repeated in the poem?

In the third stanza what are the words that express merriment? Most poems contain a deeper thought than the mere words convey. What lines in the third stanza give you a hint of the hidden thought?

Explain fully the last stanza. What is a "vacant mood"? a "pensive mood"? Give synonyms for "pensive."

What is "that inward eye"? What is the antecedent of "which" and of "they"? Is there bliss in solitude? Name some of the joys that might come to one in solitude.

Describe the stages of emotions from the first line to the last in the fourth stanza.

A GREEN CORNFIELD

[POEM FOR CLASS DISCUSSION]

A GREEN CORNFIELD

CHRISTINA GEORGINA ROSSETTI

The earth was green, the sky was blue:
   I saw and heard one sunny morn
A skylark hang between the two,
   A singing speck above the corn.

A stage below, in gay accord,
   White butterflies danced on the wing,
And still the singing skylark soared
   And silent sank and soared to sing.

The cornfield stretched a tender green
   To right and left beside my walks;
I knew he had a nest unseen
   Somewhere among the million stalks.

And as I paused to hear his song
   While swift the sunny moments slid,
Perhaps his mate sat listening long,
   And listened longer than I did.

TO DAFFODILS

Robert Herrick

Fair Daffodils, we weep to see
   You haste away so soon:
As yet the early-rising sun
   Has not attain'd his noon.
        Stay, stay,
   Until the hasting day
        Has run
   But to the even song;
And, having pray'd together, we
   Will go with you along.

We have short time to stay as you,
   We have as short a spring;
As quick a growth to meet decay,
   As you, or anything.
        We die,
   As your hours do, and dry
        Away
   Like to the summer's rain,
Or as the pearls of morning's dew
   Ne'er to be found again.

You have just studied Wordsworth's "I Wandered Lonely as a Cloud," a sprightly lyric of the nineteenth century. This poem of Herrick's is a typical seventeenth-century lyric.

To what season of the year do daffodils belong?
Are they short-lived as the poet's lines imply?

What is the meaning of "hasting"?
Do you often see the word? What do you see instead?

What do you know of the use of "even"?
What time is indicated by the "even song"?

In the second stanza, a reason is given for "having prayed together." What is the reason?

Is our life as short as that of the daffodil?
Notice how the poet emphasizes the shortness of life, — "as short a spring"; "as quick a growth to meet decay"; "we die, as your hours do, and dry away"; "like to the summer's rain"; "as the pearls of morning's dew." Continue the comparisons from nature, — in the stars, in the clouds, the wind, and so forth.

Why has the poet deliberately exaggerated "life's little span"?

Which of these two daffodil poems do you like better and why?

THE BUILDERS

[POEM FOR CLASS DISCUSSION]

THE BUILDERS

HENRY WADSWORTH LONGFELLOW

All are architects of Fate,
   Working in these walls of Time;
Some with massive deeds and great,
   Some with ornaments of rhyme.

Nothing useless is, or low;
   Each thing in its place is best;
And what seems but idle show
   Strengthens and supports the rest.

For the structure that we raise,
   Time is with materials filled;
Our to-days and yesterdays
   Are the blocks with which we build.

Truly shape and fashion these;
   Leave no yawning gaps between;
Think not, because no man sees,
   Such things will remain unseen.

In the elder days of Art,
   Builders wrought with greatest care
Each minute and unseen part;
   For the Gods see everywhere.

Let us do our work as well,
   Both the unseen and the seen;
Make the house, where Gods may dwell,
   Beautiful, entire, and clean.

Else our lives are incomplete,
   Standing in these walls of Time,
Broken stairways, where the feet
   Stumble as they seek to climb.

Build to-day, then, strong and sure,
   With a firm and ample base;
And ascending and secure
   Shall to-morrow find its place.

Thus alone can we attain
   To those turrets, where the eye
Sees the world as one vast plain,
   And one boundless reach of sky.

WYNKEN, BLYNKEN, AND NOD

Eugene Field

Wynken, Blynken, and Nod one night
   Sailed off in a wooden shoe —
Sailed on a river of crystal light,
   Into a sea of dew.
"Where are you going, and what do you wish?"
   The old moon asked the three.
"We have come to fish for the herring fish
   That live in this beautiful sea;
   Nets of silver and gold have we,"
            Said Wynken,
            Blynken,
            And Nod.

The old moon laughed and sang a song,
   As they rocked in the wooden shoe,
And the wind that sped them all night long
   Ruffled the waves of dew.
The little stars were the herring fish
   That lived in the beautiful sea —
"Now cast your nets wherever you wish —
   But never afeared are we!"

So cried the stars to the fishermen three:
    Wynken,
    Blynken,
    And Nod.

All night long their nets they threw
  For the fish in the twinkling foam —
Then down from the sky came the wooden shoe,
  Bringing the fishermen home;
'Twas all so pretty a sail it seemed
  As if it could not be,
And some folk thought 'twas a dream they'd dreamed
  Of sailing that beautiful sea —
  But I shall name you the fishermen three:
    Wynken,
    Blynken,
    And Nod.

Wynken and Blynken are two little eyes,
  And Nod is a little head,
And the wooden shoe that sailed the skies
  Is a wee one's trundle-bed.
So shut your eyes while mother sings
  Of wonderful sights that be,
And you shall see the beautiful things
  As you rock on the misty sea,

WYNKEN, BLYNKEN, AND NOD

Where the old shoe rocked the fishermen three:
Wynken,
Blynken,
And Nod.

◇ ◇ ◇

This Dutch lullaby of Eugene Field's is so dear to children and so calculated to fire the imagination that it could ill be spared from any anthology for young readers. As it is fully explained, few questions will be necessary.

Why is the phrase "crystal light" used? why "sea of dew"? Can you imagine an expanse of dew? What are the "Nets of silver and gold"?

What old myth is alluded to in "the old moon laughed and sang a song"?

What are the "waves of dew," "the herring fish," "the beautiful sea"?

What is the meaning of "afeared"?

Have you ever before heard the word used?

How long did the fishing expedition last? Why?

When did the "wooden shoe" come home?

Find other poems about "dreamland."

Who is the Sandman?

Who is Morpheus?

Find other lullaby songs. Every nation has its own form of lullaby. Field has written Japanese, Danish, Sicilian, Corsican, and other slumber songs.

What do you know of the popular Negro Spirituals?

[POEMS FOR CLASS DISCUSSION]

THE GLOVE AND THE LIONS

Leigh Hunt

King Francis was a hearty king, and loved a royal sport,
And one day, as his lions fought, sat looking on the court.
The nobles filled the benches, with the ladies in their pride,
And 'mongst them sat the Count de Lorge, with one for whom he sighed;
And truly 'twas a gallant thing to see that crowning show,
Valor and love, and a king above, and the royal beasts below.

Ramped and roared the lions, with horrid laughing jaws;
They bit, they glared, gave blows like beams, a wind went with their paws.
With wallowing might and stifled roar they rolled on one another,
Till all the pit with sand and mane was in a thunderous smother.

THE GLOVE AND THE LIONS

The bloody foam above the bars came whisking through the air;
Said Francis then, "Faith, gentlemen, we're better here than there."

De Lorge's love o'erheard the king, a beauteous, lively dame,
With smiling lips and sharp bright eyes, which always seemed the same;
She thought, "The Count, my lover, is brave as brave can be;
He surely would do wondrous things to show his love of me.
Kings, ladies, lovers, all look on; the occasion is divine.
I'll drop my glove, to prove his love. Great glory will be mine."

She dropped her glove, to prove his love, then looked at him and smiled.
He bowed, and in a moment leaped among the lions wild:
The leap was quick, return was quick, he has regained his place,
Then threw the glove, but not with love, right in the lady's face.

"By heaven," said Francis, "rightly done!" and he
    rose from where he sat;
"No love," quoth he, "but vanity, sets love a task
    like that."

BEFORE SLEEPING

An Old English Prayer

Matthew, Mark, Luke, and John,
Bless the bed that I lie on.
Before I lay me down to sleep,
I give my soul to Christ to keep.
Four corners to my bed,
Four angels there aspread,
Two to foot and two to head,
And four to carry me when I'm dead.
I go by sea, I go by land,
The Lord made me with His right hand.
If any danger come to me,
Sweet Jesus Christ, deliver me.
He's the branch and I'm the flower,
Pray God send me a happy hour,
And if I die before I wake,
I pray that Christ my soul will take.

THE LAMB

William Blake

Little Lamb, who made thee?
Dost thou know who made thee,
Gave thee life, and bade thee feed
By the stream and o'er the mead;
Gave thee clothing of delight,
Softest clothing, woolly, bright;
Gave thee such a tender voice,
Making all the vales rejoice?
Little Lamb, who made thee?
Dost thou know who made thee?

Little Lamb, I'll tell thee;
Little Lamb, I'll tell thee:
He is callèd by thy name,
For He calls Himself a Lamb.
He is meek, and He is mild,
He became a little child.
I a child, and thou a lamb,
We are callèd by His name.
Little Lamb, God bless thee!
Little Lamb, God bless thee!

Who is asking the questions of the "Little Lamb"?
Enumerate the things that have been given to the Lamb.
What gifts have you received from the same source?
Do you like the refrains at the end of each stanza? Why?
Who called our Lord a lamb? Upon what occasion?
In what qualities was Jesus like a lamb?
Are these qualities peculiar to childhood?
How did our Lord show His love for little children? In what words did He invite them to come to Him?
In what sublime sacrifice is Jesus called the "Lamb of God"?

[POEM FOR CLASS DISCUSSION]

THE TIGER

WILLIAM BLAKE

Tiger, Tiger, burning bright
In the forests of the night,
What immortal hand or eye
Could frame thy fearful symmetry?

In what distant deeps or skies
Burned the fire of thine eyes?
On what wings dare he aspire?
What the hand dare seize the fire?

THE TIGER

And what shoulder and what art
Could twist the sinews of thy heart?
And, when thy heart began to beat,
What dread hand and what dread feet?

What the hammer? what the chain?
In what furnace was thy brain?
What the anvil? what dread grasp
Dare its deadly terrors clasp?

When the stars threw down their spears,
And watered heaven with their tears,
Did he smile his work to see?
Did He who made the lamb make thee?

Tiger, Tiger, burning bright
In the forests of the night,
What immortal hand or eye
Dare frame thy fearful symmetry?

A CHILD'S THOUGHT OF GOD

Elizabeth Barrett Browning

They say that God lives very high.
   But if you look above the pines,
You cannot see our God. And why?

And if you dig down in the mines
   You never see Him in the gold;
Though, from Him, all that's glory shines.

God is so good, He wears a fold
   Of Heaven and earth across His face —
Like secrets kept, for love, untold.

But still I feel that His embrace
   Slides down by thrills, through all things made,
Through sight and sound of every place:

As if my tender mother laid
   On my shut lips, her kisses' pressure,
Half-waking me at night; and said
   "Who kissed you through the dark, dear guesser?"

In the second line, why is the pine designated rather than any other kind of tree?

Why can you not see God there or in the depth of the earth, or anywhere?

What do you think of the use of "fold" in the third stanza?

Is it more expressive than the word "veil" would be? Why?

Name some of the possible untold secrets kept for love. There are many such secrets in mother love.

When do we feel most consciously God's presence? Does not every beautiful work of nature remind us of Him?

In the last stanza, God's love is likened to a mother's affection.

Is there a sweeter memory than that of a mother's kiss in the dark, or a more perfect reminder of God's presence than is suggested in the closing line?

◇ ◇ ◇

[POEM FOR CLASS DISCUSSION]

SONG FOR A LITTLE HOUSE

CHRISTOPHER MORLEY

I'm glad our house is a little house,
    Not too tall nor too wide:
I'm glad the hovering butterflies
    Feel free to come inside.

Our little house is a friendly house,
    It is not shy or vain;
It gossips with the talking trees,
    And makes friends with the rain.

And quick leaves cast a shimmer of green
    Against our whited walls,
And in the phlox, the courteous bees
    Are paying duty calls.

THE TOYS

Coventry Patmore

My little Son, who look'd from thoughtful eyes
And moved and spoke in quiet grown-up wise,
Having my law the seventh time disobey'd,
I struck him, and dismiss'd
With hard words and unkiss'd, —
His Mother, who was patient, being dead.
Then, fearing lest his grief should hinder sleep,
I visited his bed,
But found him slumbering deep,
With darken'd eyelids, and their lashes yet
From his late sobbing wet.
And I, with moan,
Kissing away his tears, left others of my own;
For, on a table drawn beside his head,
He had put, within his reach,
A box of counters and a red-vein'd stone,
A piece of glass abraded by the beach
And six or seven shells,
A bottle with bluebells,
And two French copper coins, ranged there with
    careful art,

To comfort his sad heart.
So when that night I pray'd
To God, I wept, and said:
Ah, when at last we lie with trancèd breath,
Not vexing Thee in death,
And Thou rememberest of what toys
We made our joys,
How weakly understood
Thy great commanded good,
Then, fatherly not less
Than I whom Thou hast moulded from the clay,
Thou'lt leave Thy wrath, and say,
"I will be sorry for their childishness."

Relate the poem in your own words. Why has the poet told us that his son had "thoughtful eyes" and that he spoke in "quiet grown-up wise"?

Do those expressions reveal the character of the boy?

Had the father any unusual provocation?

How many forms of punishment did he inflict? Which was the severest to the sensitive heart?

Why has Patmore inserted the line "His Mother, who was patient, being dead"?

How would the patient mother probably have punished her disobedient child?

How did the father show his repentance for his harshness? What marks had he of the child's grief?

Why had the boy selected the toys that he had carefully placed beside him?

What comparison did the father make in his prayer?

What is "trancèd breath"? How else could the poet have expressed this thought?

Why is the accent placed over the *e* in "trancèd"?

How do we make toys of our joys?

Does the concluding line remind you of the Gospel word, "The spirit indeed is willing, but the flesh is weak"?

Why does the poet use "weakly understood"?

Could we not say of all God's precepts "Thy great commanded good"?

Express in a simpler form "whom Thou hast moulded from the clay."

Is not God's willingness to forgive our every fault an answer to this prayer of Patmore's?

What parts of the poem do you especially like? Why?

[POEM FOR CLASS DISCUSSION]

SEVEN TIMES ONE

Jean Ingelow

There's no dew left on the daisies and clover,
    There's no rain left in heaven;
I've said my "seven times" over and over,
    Seven times one are seven.

I am old, so old I can write a letter;
   My birthday lessons are done;
The lambs play always, they know no better;
   They are only one times one.

O moon! in the night I have seen you sailing
   And shining so round and low;
You were bright! ah, bright! but your light is failing, —
   You are nothing now but a bow.

You moon, have you done something wrong in heaven
   That God has hidden your face?
I hope if you have you will soon be forgiven
   And shine again in your place.

O velvet bee, you're a dusty fellow;
   You've powdered your legs with gold!
O brave marsh marybuds, rich and yellow,
   Give me your money to hold!

O columbine, open your folded wrapper,
   Where two twin turtledoves dwell!
O cuckoopint, toll me the purple clapper
   That hangs in your clear, green bell!

And show me your nest with the young ones in it, —
　　I will not steal them away;
I am old! you may trust me, linnet, linnet, —
　　I am seven times one to-day.

EPITAPH

SAMUEL TAYLOR COLERIDGE

Stop, Christian passer-by! — Stop, child of God,
And read with gentle breast. Beneath this sod
A poet lies, or that which once seem'd he.
O, lift one thought in prayer for S. T. C.;
That he who many a year with toil of breath
Found death in life, may here find life in death!
Mercy for praise — to be forgiven for fame
He ask'd, and hoped, through Christ. Do thou the
　　same!

A BALLAD OF TREES AND THE MASTER

Sidney Lanier

Into the woods my Master went,
Clean forspent, forspent.
Into the woods my Master came,
Forspent with love and shame,
But the olives they were not blind to Him;
The little gray leaves were kind to Him:
The thorn-tree had a mind to Him,
When into the woods He came.

Out of the woods my Master went,
And He was well content.
Out of the woods my Master came,
Content with death and shame.
When death and shame would woo Him last,
From under the trees they drew Him last;
'Twas on a tree they slew Him — last;
When out of the woods He came.

Read this poem aloud to see if you do not love the rhythm of it.

Notice the rhyming arrangement.

A BALLAD OF TREES AND THE MASTER

What phase of our Divine Master's Passion is here pictured?

Where are these woods?

What is the meaning of "forspent"?

Does the word "clean" add anything to the thought?

Have you ever before seen "clean" used in this sense?

What was the "love and shame" with which He was forspent?

To what, do you think, does the fifth line draw a comparison?

How were the little gray leaves kind to Him?

Why had the thorn-tree a mind to Him?

Was it to participate further in His Passion?

Do you notice that man, man alone, was unkind to Christ, and do you remember that on one occasion He referred to the stones crying out?

What wrought the change in the Master indicated in the second stanza?

Does the word "woo" in the fifth line tell you our Lord's feeling toward death and shame?

His last prayer and His last respite were under the sheltering trees. Does not that fact and the greater reality that Christ died upon a tree tell you that He must have loved trees?

Can you not see spiritual reasons why, as Kilmer says, "only God can make a tree"?

Read "Garden and Cradle," by Eugene Field, and note the resemblance to this poem.

[POEM FOR CLASS DISCUSSION]

I SEE HIS BLOOD UPON THE ROSE

Joseph Mary Plunkett

I see His blood upon the rose
   And in the stars the glory of His eyes,
His body gleams amid eternal snows,
   His tears fall from the skies.

I see His face in every flower;
   The thunder and the singing of the birds
Are but His voice — and carven by His power
   Rocks are His written words.

All pathways by His feet are worn,
   His strong heart stirs the ever-beating sea,
His crown of thorns is twined with every thorn,
   His cross is every tree.

IN THE FIELDS

[The authorship of this poem is disputed. In several anthologies it is attributed to Elizabeth Barrett Browning, but it is not found in any edition of her works and it is quite unlike her style.]

>The little cares that fretted me,
>   I lost them yesterday
>Among the fields above the sea,
>   Among the winds at play;
>Among the lowing of the herds,
>   The rustling of the trees;
>Among the singing of the birds,
>   The humming of the bees.

>The foolish fears of what might pass —
>   I cast them all away
>Among the clover-scented grass,
>   Among the new-mown hay;
>Among the husking of the corn,
>   Where drowsy poppies nod,
>Where ill thoughts die and good are born,
>   Out in the fields with God.

Are not most of the cares that fret us "little cares"?
What remedy for them does the poet give?
Enumerate the various beauties of nature that are given in the first stanza.

Name in the second stanza those that lull to rest the "foolish fears."

In both the first and the second stanza, list the things that appeal to the sight and those that appeal to other senses.

Have you ever experienced the truth of the last two lines?

Can you associate love of nature with crime?

Which are more healthful to soul and body, outdoor sports or indoor amusements?

Why are "fears of what might pass" foolish? We have a saying, "Never cross a bridge until you come to it." What does that mean?

[POEM FOR CLASS DISCUSSION]

THE IRISH

Francis Carlin

With a gentle Hand
  God made the Gael
For that fair land
  Of Innisfail,
By angels planned.

THE IRISH

A child is he
 With an agèd smile
Of mystery,
 In the oldest isle
Of an ancient sea.

And He Who made
 The Gael is kind
To the yew-tree's shade
 And the dusty wind,
Where the old are laid

In that strange land
 Of Innisfail,
By angels planned
 For the childish Gael
Who holds God's Hand.

THE SWING

Robert Louis Stevenson

How do you like to go up in a swing,
    Up in the air so blue?
Oh, I do think it the pleasantest thing
    Ever a child can do!

Up in the air and over the wall,
    Till I can see so wide,
Rivers and trees and cattle and all
    Over the country-side.

Till I look down on the garden green,
    Down on the roof so brown —
Up in the air I go flying again,
    Up in the air and down!

◇ ◇ ◇

There is so much of romance in this little poem of Stevenson's that it makes strong appeal to the imagination of children.

Have you not experienced the thrill of going high up in a swing and did you not desire to go higher and higher? Can you recall some definite incident of this kind? Relate it as clearly as you can.

Could you really see all that the second stanza describes?

What part of it is purely imaginative? Can you suggest other pictures that might come in view while swinging gayly up and down?

What is the mood of the poem?

How old is the child to whom this sport is so keen a joy?

Is the roller coaster at all akin to the old-fashioned grape swing?

[POEM FOR CLASS DISCUSSION]

"TIME, YOU OLD GIPSY MAN"[1]

RALPH HODGSON

Time, you old gipsy man,
　Will you not stay,
Put up your caravan
　Just for one day?

All things I'll give you
　Will you be my guest,

[1] Reprinted from Ralph Hodgson's *Eve and Other Poems*. By permission of The Macmillan Company.

Bells for your jennet
  Of silver the best,
Goldsmiths shall beat you
  A great golden ring,
Peacocks shall bow to you,
  Little boys sing,
Oh, and sweet girls will
  Festoon you with may.
Time, you old gipsy,
  Why hasten away?

Last week in Babylon,
  Last night in Rome,
Morning and in the crush
  Under Paul's dome;
Under Paul's dial
  You tighten your rein —
Only a moment
  And off once again;
Off to some city
  Now blind in the womb,
Off to another
  Ere that's in the tomb.

Time, you old gipsy man,
  Will you not stay,
Put up your caravan
  Just for one day?

You will love this poem, children, because it is so rhythmic and so full of imagery. Recall your old nursery jingle, "Rings on her fingers, bells on her toes." Does it have a place in this poem?

The fleeting quality of Time is emphasized throughout the stanza beginning, "Last week in Babylon, Last night in Rome." Babylon had its day and Rome and the rest, and cities yet unborn will rise and fall while Time goes hurrying on.

TO THE FRINGED GENTIAN

William Cullen Bryant

Thou blossom bright with autumn dew,
And colored with the heaven's own blue,
That openest when the quiet light
Succeeds the keen and frosty night.

Thou comest not when violets lean
O'er wandering brooks and springs unseen,
Or columbines, in purple dressed,
Nod o'er the ground-bird's hidden nest.

Thou waitest late and com'st alone,
When woods are bare and birds are flown,
And frosts and shortening days portend
The aged year is near his end.

Then doth thy sweet and quiet eye
Look through its fringes to the sky,
Blue — blue — as if that sky let fall
A flower from its cerulean wall.

I would that thus, when I shall see
The hour of death draw near to me,
Hope, blossoming within my heart,
May look to heaven as I depart.

◇ ◇ ◇

In what season of the year does the gentian appear?
Name other flowers peculiar to this season.

What qualities characterize spring flowers? autumn flowers?

Why is the expression "quiet light" used here? How would you designate summer light?

Where do the violets grow most profusely? When?
Do you know the columbine?
Why does the poet say "hidden nest"?

In the third stanza in how many different ways are you told the season of the year? Can you add other ways of telling it?

What is this "sweet and quiet eye"?
Why is the word "fringes" used?
Could the poet have used the word "lashes"? Which do you prefer?
What is the "cerulean wall"?

What does Bryant take the gentian to symbolize? Is his comparison apt?

Name other blue flowers associated with the sky in one of Longfellow's poems.

◇ ◇ ◇

[POEM FOR CLASS DISCUSSION]

THE GREEN O' THE SPRING

Denis A. McCarthy

Sure, afther all the winther,
   An' afther all the snow,
'T is fine to see the sunshine,
   'T is fine to feel its glow;
'T is fine to see the buds break
   On boughs that bare have been —
But best of all to Irish eyes
   'T is grand to see the green!

Sure, afther all the winther,
   An' afther all the snow,
'T is fine to hear the brooks sing
   As on their way they go;
'T is fine to hear at mornin'
   The voice of robineen,
But best of all to Irish eyes
   'T is grand to see the green!

Sure, here in grim New England
  The spring is always slow,
An' every bit o' green grass
  Is kilt wid frost and snow;
Ah, many a heart is weary
  The winther days, I ween
But oh, the joy when springtime comes
  An' brings the blessed green!

THE MAN OF THE HOUSE

Katharine Tynan

Joseph, honoured from sea to sea,
This is your name that pleases me,
   "Man of the House."

I see you rise at the dawn and light
The fire and blow till the flame is bright.

I see you take the pitcher and carry
The deep well-water for Jesus and Mary.

You knead the corn for the bread so fine,
Gather them grapes from the hanging vine.

There are little feet that are soft and slow,
Follow you whithersoever you go.

There's a little face at your workshop door,
A little one sits down on your floor:

Holds His hands for the shavings curled,
The soft little hands that have made the world

Mary calls you: the meal is ready:
You swing the Child to your shoulder steady.

I see your quiet smile as you sit
And watch the little Son thrive and eat.

The vine curls by the window space,
The wings of angels cover the face.

Up in the rafters, polished and olden,
There's a Dove that broods and his wings are golden.

You who kept Them through shine and storm,
A staff, a shelter kindly and warm,

Father of Jesus, husband of Mary,
Hold us your lilies for sanctuary!

Joseph, honoured from sea to sea,
Guard me mine and my own rooftree,
        "Man of the House"!

   Who are the Josephs that you know from Bible history? What is all that the Sacred Scripture says of this Joseph?

THE MAN OF THE HOUSE

Enumerate the things that Joseph did for his family. Are these the things commonly done today by the man of the house?

What are some of the household improvements of the twentieth century?

Are not the actions of the Child Jesus much the same as those of any other child? Notice that He follows St. Joseph about his workshop, that He sits down on the floor, that He holds up His hands for the shaving curls, that He likes to be swung to His foster father's shoulders.

The natural beauty of a growing vine is seen in the window space, but what covers the facing above? What is the office of these holy spirits?

What is the "Dove" that broods over the Holy Family?

In the early ages of Christianity and on through the Middle Ages the sanctuary was a safe refuge for fugitives from justice. What is the force of "lilies for sanctuary," taking lilies as a symbol of St. Joseph's spotless purity?

What is the significance of "rooftree"? Do you like the word?

[POEM FOR CLASS DISCUSSION]

MARY IMMACULATE

Eleanor C. Donnelly

"Pure as the snow," we say. Ah! never flake
  Fell through the air
  One-tenth as fair
As Mary's soul was made for Christ's dear sake.
  Virgin Immaculate,
The whitest whiteness of the Alpine snows,
Beside thy stainless spirit, dusky grows.

"Pure as the stars." Ah! never lovely night
  Wore in its diadem
  So pure a gem
As that which fills the ages with its light.
  Virgin Immaculate,
The peerless splendors of thy soul by far
Outshine the glow of heaven's serenest star.

FOR THOSE WHO FAIL [1]

Joaquin Miller

"All honor to him who shall win the prize,"
    The world has cried for a thousand years;
But to him who tries and who fails and dies,
    I give great honor and glory and tears.

. . . .

O, great is the hero who wins a name,
    But greater many and many a time,
Some pale-faced fellow who dies in shame,
    And lets God finish the thought sublime.

And great is the man with a sword undrawn,
    And good is the man who refrains from wine;
But the man who fails and yet fights on,
    Lo! he is the twin-born brother of mine!

◇ ◇ ◇

The Americans are the greatest of hero worshipers. Recall incidents and persons to whom the first line of this poem is applicable.

[1] Permission to use this poem granted by the Harr Wagner Publishing Company, publishers of Joaquin Miller's *Complete Poems*.

How does the world look upon "him who tries and who fails"?

From a worldly point of view was not our Divine Saviour, dying a malefactor's death, a failure?

What, then, is success, measured by God's standard?

Can you recall from history concrete examples of the two heroes described in the second stanza?

As a rule, do men who achieve greatness see the results? Name from history some that have gone to their graves in poverty or perhaps in disgrace, but whose names are now emblazoned in the hall of fame?

Explain the meaning of "the man with a sword undrawn."

What virtue is extolled in the second line of the last stanza?

It takes heroic courage to fight on in the face of repeated failure; but this dual nature of strength and weakness, inherent in all humanity, makes every man twin brother to his fellow man.

[POEM FOR CLASS DISCUSSION]

"WHAT IS IN HEAVEN?"

Richard Rolle

"There is life without any death,
  And there is youth without any elde,
  And there is all manner of wealth to welde,

"WHAT IS IN HEAVEN?"

There is rest without any travaille,
And there is peace without any strife,
And there is all manner of joy of life,
And there is bright summer ever to see,
And there is never winter in that country,
And there is gret melody of angel song,
And there is praising them among,
And there is ever perfect love and charity,
And there is wisdom without folly."

        elde: age
        welde: manage
        travaille: labor
        gret: great

THE MAGNIFICAT

St. Luke (i, 46-55)

My soul doth magnify the Lord.

And my spirit hath rejoiced in God my Saviour.

Because he hath regarded the humility of his handmaid; for behold from henceforth all generations shall call me blessed.

Because he that is mighty, hath done great things to me; and holy is his name.

And his mercy is from generation unto generations, to them that fear him.

He hath showed might in his arm; he hath scattered the proud in the conceit of their heart.

He hath put down the mighty from their seat, and hath exalted the humble.

He hath filled the hungry with good things; and the rich he hath sent empty away.

He hath received Israel his servant, being mindful of his mercy:

As he spoke to our fathers, to Abraham and to his seed for ever.

THE MAGNIFICAT

Who uttered this beautiful lyric and upon what occasion?

What especial reason is given for this canticle of praise?

What is a handmaid?

We may regard as prophetic the words "all generations shall call me blessed." How has this prophecy been fulfilled?

To whom does the canticle refer all praise?

What great things are alluded to in the fourth verse?

What great things hath He done for all of us through this humble handmaid?

Why is the word "fear" used in the fifth verse?

Could you substitute "love"?

What are the "mercies" enumerated?

Do you recall any words or any parable of our Lord reminding us of the line "He hath put down the mighty from their seat, and hath exalted the humble"?

The verse which follows this line calls to mind the parable of Dives and Lazarus. Tell how it does so.

Who is "his servant Israel"?

What promise did God make to Abraham? How and when was it accomplished?

[POEM FOR CLASS DISCUSSION]

AN OLD CHRISTMAS CAROL

I saw three ships come sailing in
  On Christmas Day, on Christmas Day,
I saw three ships come sailing in
  On Christmas Day in the morning.

And what was in those ships all three
  On Christmas Day, on Christmas Day?
And what was in those ships all three
  On Christmas Day in the morning?

Our Saviour Christ and His Ladye,
  On Christmas Day, on Christmas Day,
Our Saviour Christ and His Ladye,
  On Christmas Day in the morning.

And whither sailed those ships all three
  On Christmas Day, on Christmas Day?
And whither sailed those ships all three
  On Christmas Day in the morning?

Oh, they sailed into Bethlehem
  On Christmas Day, on Christmas Day,
Oh, they sailed into Bethlehem
  On Christmas Day in the morning.

A CHILD'S WISH

Abram J. Ryan

I wish I were the little key
   That locks Love's Captive in,
And lets Him out to go and free
   A sinful heart from sin.

I wish I were the little bell
   That tinkles for the Host,
When God comes down each day to dwell
   With hearts He loves the most.

I wish I were the chalice fair,
   That holds the Blood of Love,
When every gleam lights holy prayer
   Upon its way above.

I wish I were the little flower
   So near the Host's sweet face,
Or like the light that half an hour
   Burns on the shrine of grace.

> I wish I were the altar where,
>   As on His mother's breast,
> Christ nestles, like a child, fore'er
>   In Eucharistic rest.
>
> But, oh, my God, I wish the most
>   That my poor heart may be
> A home all holy for each Host
>   That comes in love to me.

◇ ◇ ◇

Childhood is the time for fairy wishes and foolish wishes, but also for very lovely wishes. Father Ryan's little poem is full of lovely wishes. Which of the wishes is the dearest to the heart of Christ? Who is "Love's Captive"? What is His prison? From what kind of sin will "Love's Captive" free us? Give a reason for your answer.

When is the bell rung?
How often is it rung during the Mass?

What does the chalice hold at the beginning of the Mass?
What holds the Host?
To what does "gleam" refer? How does it light holy prayer?

Why is "sweet face" used in reference to the Host?
Why is the time limited to half an hour?

Do you especially like the fifth stanza? Why?

Does it give you a very definite idea of our Eucharistic Lord?

The last stanza brings the wish into the personal life of each of us. The other wishes are symbolic of the preparation each heart should make to be worthy to receive Christ in Holy Communion. Try to explain the symbolism in each wish.

◇ ◇ ◇

[POEM FOR CLASS DISCUSSION]

AN OLD WOMAN'S ROSARY

Hugh F. Blunt

I bless myself, and I kiss the Cross,
    And the holy Creed I tell,
And the Paters and Aves trip off my tongue
    For it's me that knows them well.

For it's many a day these same old beads,
    I've told in the same old way,
I got them my First Communion morn,
    And that's sixty years this May.

'Twas the joyful mysteries then I liked,
    (And I said them joyfully),
When Our Lord was only a Child himself,
    At his Blessed Mother's knee.

Ochone! but it's many and many a year,
    I've turned from the joyful deeds,
And I cry on the sorrowful mysteries,
    With tears as big as my beads.

For my beautiful boy with the fever went,
    And "himself" next morning died,
Do you wonder I think of the mysteries,
    That end with the Crucified?

For it's them I'm telling each blessèd bead,
    A-kneeling beside my bed.
We two women, God's Mother and me,
    Have many a talk of our dead.

And that's why I'm liking the beads that tell
    Her pains and her darling Son's.
It's plenty of time I'll be having in Heaven,
    To think of the glorious ones.

THE DAY IS DONE

Henry Wadsworth Longfellow

The day is done, and the darkness
   Falls from the wings of Night,
As a feather is wafted downward
   From an eagle in his flight.

I see the lights of the village
   Gleam through the rain and the mist,
And a feeling of sadness comes o'er me
   That my soul cannot resist:

A feeling of sadness and longing,
   That is not akin to pain,
And resembles sorrow only
   As the mist resembles the rain.

Come, read to me some poem,
   Some simple and heartfelt lay,
That shall soothe this restless feeling,
   And banish the thoughts of day.

Not from the grand old masters,
   Not from the bards sublime,
Whose distant footsteps echo
   Through the corridors of Time.

For, like strains of martial music,
   Their mighty thoughts suggest
Life's endless toil and endeavor;
   And to-night I long for rest.

Read from some humbler poet,
   Whose songs gushed from his heart,
As showers from the clouds of summer,
   Or tears from the eyelids start;

Who, through long days of labor,
   And nights devoid of ease,
Still heard in his soul the music
   Of wonderful melodies.

Such songs have power to quiet
   The restless pulse of care,
And come like the benediction
   That follows after prayer.

Then read from the treasured volume
   The poem of thy choice,
And lend to the rhyme of the poet
   The beauty of thy voice.

THE DAY IS DONE

And the night shall be filled with music,
And the cares, that infest the day,
Shall fold their tents, like the Arabs,
And as silently steal away.

Longfellow in the first stanza of "The Day is Done" describes the coming of night, "As a feather is wafted downward." Is not that coming swift and noiseless? Are these characteristic qualities? In "The Children's Hour," how does this poet describe twilight? Can you find other pictures of nightfall?

Should weather conditions affect our spirits? Why?
Was the poet's feeling caused by the rain?
How does the mist resemble the rain?

In the fourth stanza the poet gives the reason for his sadness. What is it?
What remedy does he suggest for his restlessness?
Why does he not wish to hear the great masterpieces, or military music?
What effect has the hearing of our national airs, — of "The Star-Spangled Banner" for instance?
What reason does the poet give for desiring the lays of some humbler poet?
How do showers come from the clouds of summer?
Is the comparison to tears apt?
Is it possible to hear or feel in the soul "the music Of wonderful melodies" despite labor and suffering?

Do you not think that music or poetry born of suffering would be most likely to soothe the restless soul?

What is the benediction that follows after prayer?

To whom is the poet talking in the tenth stanza?

What kind of music is it that would fill the night and drive away care?

What is the reference here to the Arabs? What do you know about these people?

[POEMS FOR CLASS DISCUSSION]

SWEET AND LOW

Alfred Tennyson

Sweet and low, sweet and low,
    Wind of the western sea,
Low, low, breathe and blow,
    Wind of the western sea!
Over the rolling waters go,
Come from the dying moon, and blow,
    Blow him again to me;
While my little one, while my pretty one, sleeps.

    Sleep and rest, sleep and rest,
        Father will come to thee soon;
    Rest, rest, on mother's breast,
        Father will come to thee soon;

Father will come to his babe in the nest,
Silver sails all out of the west
  Under the silver moon;
Sleep, my little one, sleep, my pretty one, sleep.

◇ ◇ ◇

I WALKED A MILE

John B. Tabb

I walked a mile with Pleasure,
  She chatted all the way,
But left me none the wiser
  For all she had to say.

I walked a mile with Sorrow,
  And not a word said she,
But oh, the things I learned from her,
  When Sorrow walked with me.

THE QUALITY OF MERCY

William Shakespeare

The quality of mercy is not strain'd;
It droppeth as the gentle rain from heaven
Upon the place beneath: it is twice bless'd;
It blesseth him that gives, and him that takes:
'Tis mightiest in the mightiest: it becomes
The thronèd monarch better than his crown:
His sceptre shows the force of temporal power,
The attribute to awe and majesty,
Wherein doth sit the dread and fear of kings;
But mercy is above this sceptred sway:
It is enthronèd in the hearts of kings;
It is an attribute to God himself;
And earthly power doth then show likest God's
When mercy seasons justice.

"The Merchant of Venice," Act IV, Scene i

Tell the class the story of "The Merchant of Venice," from which this selection is taken, and the occasion upon which these words were uttered.

When is a thing strained? Does the second line carry out the same idea?

What other word could have been used instead of "droppeth"? Name some of the ways in which rain comes down.

Is it true that the merciful are "twice bless'd"? How? Someone has said, "Virtue is its own reward." Do you think this true?

The poet explains his own lines: "'Tis mightiest in the mightiest: it becomes The thronèd monarch better than his crown." How does he do so?

Give instances from history of kings who were distinguished for their mercy. Do you remember one in the Old Testament who showed mercy to his intended murderer?

Why is mercy above temporal greatness? Explain "earthly power doth then show likest God's When mercy seasons justice."

What is your opinion of the lady who spoke all these lines? Should you not like to read all of "The Merchant of Venice"?

[POEM FOR CLASS DISCUSSION]

COURTESY

Hilaire Belloc

Of Courtesy, it is much less
Than Courage of Heart or Holiness,
Yet in my Walks it seems to me
That the Grace of God is in Courtesy.

On Monks I did in Storrington fall,
They took me straight into their Hall;
I saw Three Pictures on a wall,
And Courtesy was in them all.

The first Annunciation;
The second the Visitation;
The third the Consolation,
Of God that was Our Lady's Son.

The first was of Saint Gabriel;
On Wings a-flame from Heaven he fell;
And as he went upon one knee
He shone with Heavenly Courtesy.

Our Lady out of Nazareth rode —
It was her month of heavy load;
Yet was Her face both great and kind,
For Courtesy was in Her Mind.

COURTESY

The third it was our Little Lord,
Whom all the Kings in arms adored;
He was so small you could not see
His large intent of Courtesy.

Our Lord, that was Our Lady's Son,
Go bless you, People, one by one;
My Rhyme is written, my work is done.

CHARITY

Robert Burns

Who made the heart, 'tis He alone
Decidedly can try us;
He knows each chord, — its various tone,
Each spring, — its various bias:
Then at the balance let's be mute,
We never can adjust it;
What's done we partly may compute,
But know not what's resisted.

◇ ◇ ◇

Who is it that alone can know the human heart with all its emotions?

In what sense is the word "try" used here?

What are the chords and the spring of the heart?

When do we take the balance in hand? Why can we never adjust it?

God sees the intention, man sees only the action. Which counts before God? Is this an explanation of the last two lines?

Can you recall instances of mistaken judgment that caused great suffering to the victim?

Complete the quotation "And now there remain faith, hope, and charity, these three—"

[POEM FOR CLASS DISCUSSION]

ABOU BEN ADHEM

Leigh Hunt

Abou Ben Adhem (may his tribe increase!)
Awoke one night from a deep dream of peace,
And saw, within the moonlight in his room,
Making it rich and like a lily in bloom,
An Angel writing in a book of gold.
Exceeding peace had made Ben Adhem bold,
And to the Presence in the room he said,
"What writest thou?" The Vision raised its head,
And, with a look made of all sweet accord,
Answered, "The names of those who love the Lord."
"And is mine one?" said Abou. "Nay, not so,"
Replied the Angel. Abou spoke more low,
But cheerly still; and said, "I pray thee, then,
Write me as one that loves his fellow-men."

The Angel wrote, and vanished. The next night
It came again, with a great wakening light,
And showed the names whom love of God had blessed;
And, lo! Ben Adhem's name led all the rest.

JUSTICE

William Shakespeare

What stronger breastplate than a heart untainted!
Thrice is he arm'd that hath his quarrel just,
And he but naked, though lock'd up in steel,
Whose conscience with injustice is corrupted.

"Henry VI, Part II," Act III, Scene ii

◇ ◇ ◇

What is a breastplate? Is it used in modern warfare? Job has said, "The life of man upon earth is a warfare." What is the shield that we should carry in this fight?

What is the threefold armor of him whose quarrel is just? Could it not be God, his conscience, and his cause?

Tell how one can be naked, though girt with steel?

Is it true that "conscience does make cowards of us all"?

How do these lines get the title "Justice"?

In the New Testament two men beloved of God are praised for their justice. Who are they?

[POEM FOR CLASS DISCUSSION]

THE CONFESSIONAL

Helen Parry Eden

My Sorrow diligent would sweep
That dingy room infest
With dust (thereby I mean my soul)
Because she hath a Guest
Who doth require that self-same room
Be garnished for His rest.

And Sorrow (who had washed His feet
Where He before had been)
Took the long broom of Memory
And swept the corners clean,
Till in the midst of the fair floor
The sum of dust was seen.

It lay there, settled by her tears,
That fell the while she swept —
Light fluffs of grey and earthly dregs;
And over these she wept,
For all were come since last her Guest
Within the room had slept.

And, for nor broom nor tears had power
To lift the clods of ill,

She called one servant of her Guest
Who came with right good will,
For, by his sweet Lord's bidding, he
Waiteth on Sorrow still;

So, seeing she had done her part
As far as in her lay
And had intent to keep the place
More cleanly from that day,
Did with his Master's dust-pan come
And take the dust away.

She thanked him, and Him who sent
Such succor, and she spread
Fair sheets of Thankfulness and Love
Upon her Master's bed,
Then on the new-scoured threshold stood
And listened for His tread.

OUT OF BOUNDS

John B. Tabb

A little Boy of Heavenly birth,
    But far from home to-day,
Comes down to find His ball, the earth,
    That sin has cast away.
O comrades, let us one and all
Join in to get Him back His ball!

Who is this little Boy?
In what sense is He far from home?
Do you like hearing the earth called His ball? Why?
How has sin cast it away?
What did sin do to the little Boy when He grew up?
Whose sin? What does sin do to Him now?
How is the word "comrades" used?
How may we help to get Him back His ball?

What part in this game are the Foreign Mission workers playing?

[POEM FOR CLASS DISCUSSION]

THE WAY OF THE CROSS

LEONARD FEENEY, S. J.

Along the dark aisles
Of a chapel dim,
The little lame girl
Drags her withered limb.

And all alone she searches
The shadows on the walls
To find the three pictures
Where Jesus falls.

JUBILATE DEO

Psalm 99

Sing joyfully to God, all the earth: serve ye the Lord with gladness.

Come in before his presence with exceeding great joy.

Know ye that the Lord he is God: he made us, and not we ourselves.

We are his people and the sheep of his pasture. Go ye into his gates with praise, into his courts with hymns: and give glory to him.

Praise ye his name: for the Lord is sweet, his mercy endureth for ever, and his truth to generation and generation.

Who wrote the Psalms? Are all of them as joyful as this one?

What are the themes of some of the Psalms?

Are all songs joyful in spirit?

Why are joy and gladness emphasized throughout this psalm?

Has another text, "God loveth a cheerful giver," close relationship with this hymn?

What effect on the soul has the constant remembrance of God as Creator? as Father? as Redeemer? as Friend?

Does the phrase "sheep of his pasture" strengthen the assertion that "We are his people"? Do you not remember that Christ called Himself the *Good Shepherd*?
What parable explains this title?
What are the gates and the courts of the Lord?

What beautiful attributes of God are enumerated in the last verse?

Throughout the Psalms the mercy of God is extolled. Can you give a definite reason why this is so?
Are the Psalms used in the liturgy of the Church?

[POEM FOR CLASS DISCUSSION]

TO-DAY

Thomas Carlyle

So here hath been dawning
    Another blue day:
Think! wilt thou let it
    Slip useless away?

TO-DAY

Out of Eternity
   This new day is born;
Into Eternity
   At night will return.

Behold it aforetime
   No eye ever did;
So soon it forever
   From all eyes is hid.

Here hath been dawning
   Another blue day:
Think! wilt thou let it
   Slip useless away?

FATHER DAMIEN

John B. Tabb

O God, the cleanest offering
   Of tainted earth below,
Unblushing to Thy feet we bring —
   "A leper white as snow!"

◇ ◇ ◇

Who was Father Damien?
What is a leper?
Find out all you can about the leper colony at Molokai.
Is there such a colony in the United States?

Why is the word "cleanest" used here? Do you remember from your Bible history the fate of lepers at the "coming of Christ"?

What was the offering made to God in the Old Law?
Would a leper have been considered fit to offer to God?
Is this a reason for the use of "unblushing"?
Justify the use of "tainted earth."
Who was this "leper white as snow"? Why "white as snow"?

Relate the cure of the lepers as told by St. Matthew (viii) and St. Luke (xvii).

[POEMS FOR CLASS DISCUSSION]

A BUNCH OF ROSES

John B. Tabb

The rosy mouth and rosy toe
  Of little baby brother,
Until about a month ago
  Had never met each other;
But nowadays the neighbors sweet,
  In every sort of weather,
Half way with rosy fingers meet,
  To kiss and play together.

THE TAX–GATHERER

John B. Tabb

"And pray, who are you?"
Said the violet blue
To the Bee, with surprise
At his wonderful size,
In her eye-glass of dew.

"I, madam," quoth he,
"Am a publican Bee,
Collecting the tax
On honey and wax.
Have you nothing for me?"

IN FLANDERS FIELDS

John D. McCrae

In Flanders fields the poppies blow
Between the crosses, row on row,
   That mark our place; and in the sky
   The larks, still bravely singing, fly,
Scarce heard amid the guns below.

We are the Dead. Short days ago
We lived, felt dawn, saw sunset glow,
   Loved and were loved, and now we lie
      In Flanders fields.

Take up our quarrel with the foe;
To you from failing hands we throw
   The torch; be yours to hold it high.
   If ye break faith with us who die
We shall not sleep, though poppies grow
      In Flanders fields.

Where are Flanders fields?
Are poppies abundant there?
What are "the crosses, row on row"?

Why is the phrase "bravely singing" used? Is there cause for bravery on the part of even the birds?

Who are these "Dead"? What other indications of energy did they display "Short days ago"? Tell something of their manner of life at that time.

Why did the dead ask that their quarrel with the foe be continued? Does it seem to justify their cause?

In America what does the "torch" signify? What, then, is the meaning of "be yours to hold it high"?

Is there a connection between sleep and poppies? What is made from poppies?

[POEM FOR CLASS DISCUSSION]

HOHENLINDEN

Thomas Campbell

On Linden, when the sun was low,
All bloodless lay the untrodden snow,
And dark as winter was the flow
Of Iser, rolling rapidly.

But Linden saw another sight,
When the drum beat, at dead of night,
Commanding fires of death to light
The darkness of her scenery.

HOHENLINDEN

By torch and trumpet fast arrayed,
Each horseman drew his battle blade,
And furious every charger neighed,
To join the dreadful revelry.

Then shook the hills with thunder riven,
Then rushed the steed to battle driven,
And louder than the bolts of heaven,
Far flashed the red artillery.

But redder yet that light shall glow
On Linden's hills of stainèd snow,
And bloodier yet the torrent flow
Of Iser, rolling rapidly.

'Tis morn, but scarce yon level sun
Can pierce the war clouds, rolling dun,
Where furious Frank and fiery Hun
Shout in their sulphurous canopy.

The combat deepens. On, ye brave,
Who rush to glory, or the grave!
Wave, Munich! all thy banners wave,
And charge with all thy chivalry!

Few, few, shall part where many meet!
The snow shall be their winding sheet,
And every turf beneath their feet
Shall be a soldier's sepulcher.

THE RHODORA

Ralph Waldo Emerson

In May, when sea winds pierced our solitudes,
I found the fresh Rhodora in the woods,
Spreading its leafless blooms in a damp nook,
To please the desert and the sluggish brook.
The purple petals, fallen in the pool,
Made the black water with their beauty gay;
Here might the redbird come his plumes to cool,
And court the flower that cheapens his array.
Rhodora! if the sages ask thee why
This charm is wasted on the earth and sky,
Tell them, dear, that if eyes were made for seeing,
Then Beauty is its own excuse for being:
Why thou wert there, O rival of the rose!
I never thought to ask, I never knew;
But, in my simple ignorance, suppose
The self-same Power that brought me there brought
    you.

◇ ◇ ◇

    The rhodora is a plant similar to the rhododendron that grows profusely in New England during the springtime.
    Are you familiar with this beautiful flower?

Is it found only in the woods?
Is it a small plant, a shrub, or a tree?
The redbird has very beautiful plumage and coloring.
Do you really think the rhodora "cheapens his array"?

Give the stanza in Gray's "Elegy" that reminds you of this line of the poem you are studying, "This charm is wasted on the earth and sky."
Are the beauties of nature ever wasted? Why not?
Since all beauty emanates from God, does it need excuse for being?
For whom were all created things brought forth from nothing? How do the flowers fulfill their destined end?
What state has chosen the rhododendron for its representative flower?

[POEM FOR CLASS DISCUSSION]

THE BURIAL OF SIR JOHN MOORE

CHARLES WOLFE

Not a drum was heard, not a funeral note,
   As his corse to the rampart we hurried;
Not a soldier discharged his farewell shot
   O'er the grave where our hero we buried.

We buried him darkly at dead of night,
   The sods with our bayonets turning;
By the struggling moonbeam's misty light
   And the lantern dimly burning.

No useless coffin enclosed his breast,
  Not in sheet nor in shroud we wound him;
But he lay like a warrior taking his rest
  With his martial cloak around him.

Few and short were the prayers we said,
  And we spoke not a word of sorrow,
But we steadfastly gazed on the face that was dead,
  And we bitterly thought of the morrow.

We thought, as we hollowed his narrow bed,
  And smoothed down his lonely pillow,
That the foe and the stranger would tread o'er his head,
  And we far away on the billow!

Lightly they'll talk of the spirit that's gone
  And o'er his cold ashes upbraid him;
But little he'll reck, if they let him sleep on
  In the grave where a Briton has laid him.

But half of our heavy task was done
  When the clock struck the hour for retiring;
And we heard the distant and random gun
  That the foe was sullenly firing.

Slowly and sadly we laid him down,
  From the field of his fame fresh and gory;
We carved not a line and we raised not a stone,
  But we left him alone with his glory.

SONG OF THE ANGEL[1]

John Henry Newman

Softly and gently, dearly-ransom'd soul,
  In my most loving arms I now enfold thee,
And, o'er the penal waters, as they roll,
  I poise thee, and I lower thee, and hold thee.

And carefully I dip thee in the lake,
  And thou, without a sob or a resistance,
Dost through the flood thy rapid passage take,
  Sinking deep, deeper, into the dim distance.

Angels, to whom the willing task is given,
  Shall tend, and nurse, and lull thee, as thou liest;
And masses on the earth, and prayers in heaven,
  Shall aid thee at the Throne of the Most Highest.

Farewell, but not for ever! brother dear,
  Be brave and patient on thy bed of sorrow;
Swiftly shall pass thy night of trial here,
  And I will come and wake thee on the morrow.

---

[1] From "The Dream of Gerontius" in *Verses on Various Occasions*, by John Henry Cardinal Newman. By permission of the publishers, Longmans, Green & Co.

The above stanzas are the closing lines of Cardinal Newman's well-known "Dream of Gerontius." It is the Guardian Angel who speaks to the soul he has so carefully guided and protected through the years of earthly strife.

Why is the soul "dearly-ransom'd"?

What are the "penal waters"?

Why are they called "waters"? Does this accord with Scripture?

Why should there be "sob" or "resistance"?

What do you think of the use of "waters," "lake," and "flood" to express intensity of punishment?

The third stanza gives a glimpse of the beauty of our doctrine of the "Communion of Saints."

What do you call the three divisions of the Church thus united?

What is the "night of trial"?

Is "morrow" used in its literal sense, or is its use figurative?

[POEM FOR CLASS DISCUSSION]

AVE MARIA BELLS

Charles Warren Stoddard

At dawn, the joyful choir of bells,
In consecrated citadels,
Flings on the sweet and drowsy air
A brief, melodious call to prayer;
For Mary, Virgin meek and lowly,
Conceived of the Spirit Holy,
As the Lord's angel did declare.

At noon, above the fretful street,
Our souls are lifted to repeat
The prayer, with low and wistful voice:
"According to thy word and choice,
Though sorrowful and heavy laden,
So be it done to thy Handmaiden";
Then all the sacred bells rejoice.

At eve with roses in the west,
The daylight's withering bequest,
Ring, prayerful bells, while blossom bright
The stars, the lilies of the night:
Of all the songs the years have sung us,
"The Word made Flesh had dwelt among us,"
Is still our ever-new delight.

THE SHEPHERDESS

Alice Meynell

She walks — the lady of my delight —
    A shepherdess of sheep.
Her flocks are thoughts. She keeps them white;
    She guards them from the steep;
She feeds them on the fragrant height,
    And folds them in for sleep.

She roams maternal hills and bright,
    Dark valleys safe and deep.
Into that tender breast at night
    The chastest stars may peep.
She walks — the lady of my delight —
    A shepherdess of sheep.

She holds her little thoughts in sight,
    Though gay they run and leap.
She is so circumspect and right;
    She has her soul to keep.
She walks — the lady of my delight —
    A shepherdess of sheep.

THE SHEPHERDESS

The theme of this beautiful poem is chastity. Why is the lady "A shepherdess of sheep"?
Why are the flocks "thoughts"?
How can one guard one's thoughts?
What is the "fragrant height" on which they feed?
Is there a special reason for folding them in for sleep?

Can you think of a reason for the use of the word "maternal"?
Notice the contrast between bright hills and dark valleys.
Can you account for the contrast?
Why may the chastest stars peep into that tender breast at night?

How can one hold one's "thoughts in sight"?
Does not "gay they run and leap" tell you that innocent amusement is perfectly compatible with goodness?
Who are the happiest people in the world?
Are those whose lives are spent in the penance and mortification of the cloister sad or gloomy?
What is the meaning of "her soul to keep"?
What is the reward promised by our Lord to the chaste of heart?

[POEM FOR CLASS DISCUSSION]

THE HOUSEWIFE'S PRAYER

Blanche Mary Kelly

Lady, who with tender word
Didst keep the house of Christ the Lord,
Who didst set forth the bread and wine
Before the Living Wheat and Vine,
Reverently didst make the bed
Whereon was laid the holy Head
That such a cruel pillow prest
For our behoof, on Calvary's crest;
Be beside me while I go
About my labors to and fro.
Speed the wheel and speed the loom,
Guide the needle and the broom,
Make my bread rise sweet and light,
Make my cheese come foamy white,
Yellow may my butter be
As cowslips blowing on the lea.
Homely though my tasks and small,
Be beside me at them all.
Then when I shall stand to face
Jesu in the judgment place,
To me thy gracious help afford,
Who art the Handmaid of the Lord.

LITTLE BOY BLUE

Eugene Field

The little toy dog is covered with dust,
    But sturdy and staunch he stands;
The little toy soldier is red with rust,
    And his musket moulds in his hands.
Time was when the little toy dog was new
    And the soldier was passing fair,
And that was the time when our Little Boy Blue
    Kissed them and put them there.

"Now don't you go till I come," he said,
    "And don't you make any noise!"
So toddling off to his trundle-bed
    He dreamt of the pretty toys.
And as he was dreaming, an angel song
    Awakened our Little Boy Blue, —
Oh, the years are many, the years are long,
    But the little toy friends are true.

Ay, faithful to Little Boy Blue they stand,
    Each in the same old place,
Awaiting the touch of a little hand,
    The smile of a little face.

And they wonder, as waiting these long years through,
   In the dust of that little chair,
What has become of our Little Boy Blue
   Since he kissed them and put them there.

◇ ◇ ◇

Children, real children, love the toys of their younger days.

Name those of the Little Boy Blue.

From the hints in the poem, what sort of boy was this little boy?

What is the probable reason for designating him Boy Blue?

How old do you picture him?

What two age suggestions do you get?

Tell in other words what happened to Little Boy Blue.

What proofs of the fidelity of the little toys are given?

There is a figure of speech called personification which attributes life to inanimate things. How often is this figure used in the last stanza?

Does it add to the beauty of the poem?

Why does the poet emphasize the fact that "the little toy friends are true"?

Is there not much truth in the old adage, "Out of sight, out of mind"?

What does Shakespeare say of its hurt in "Blow, blow, thou winter wind"?

[POEM FOR CLASS DISCUSSION]

DA LEETLA BOY

Thomas Augustine Daly

Da spreeng ees com'! but oh, da joy
    Eet ees too late!
He was so cold, my leetla boy,
    He no could wait.

I no can count how manny week,
How manny day, dat he ees seeck;
How manny night I seet an' hold
Da leetla hand dat was so cold.
He was so patience, oh, so sweet!
Eet hurts my throat for theenk of eet;
An' all he evra ask ees w'en
Ees gona com' da spreeng agen.
Wan day, wan brighta sunny day,
He sees, across da alley way,
Da leetla girl dat's livin' dere
Ees raise her window for da air,
An' put outside a leetla pot
Of — w'at-you-call? — forgat-me-not.
So smalla flower, so leetla theeng!
But steel eet mak' hees hearta seeng:
"Oh, now, at las', ees com' da spreeng!

Da leetla plant ees glad for know
Da sun ees com' for mak' eet grow.
So, too, I am grow warm and strong."
So lika dat he seeng hees song.
But, ah! da night com' down an' den
Da weenter ees sneak back agen,
An' een da alley all da night
Ees fall da snow, so cold, so white,
An' cover up da leetla pot
Of — w'at-you-call? — forgat-me-not.
All night da leetla hand I hold
Ees grow so cold, so cold, so cold!

Da spreeng ees com'; but oh, da joy
   Eet ees too late!
He was so cold, my leetla boy,
   He no could wait.

"BREAK, BREAK, BREAK"

Alfred Tennyson

Break, break, break,
  On thy cold grey stones, O Sea!
And I would that my tongue could utter
  The thoughts that arise in me.

O well for the fisherman's boy,
  That he shouts with his sister at play!
O well for the sailor lad,
  That he sings in his boat on the bay!

And the stately ships go on
  To their haven under the hill;
But O for the touch of a vanish'd hand,
  And the sound of a voice that is still!

Break, break, break,
  At the foot of thy crags, O Sea!
But the tender grace of a day that is dead
  Will never come back to me.

Tennyson's nature was thoughtful and melancholy. Of him it was said that his Good Friday never had an Easter. Explain what that means. Does it define the mood of this beautiful lyric?

Would the "thoughts," if uttered, be gay or sorrowful?

What is the bright spot in the poem?

Why is it well for the fisher boy to shout and play and for the sailor lad to sing?

What do the "stately ships" have to do with the last two lines in the third stanza? May they not at some time have carried as part of their precious cargo the one for whom the poet sighs?

When the waves break on the shore, what becomes of them? Do you see the comparison between the waves and a day that is gone to return nevermore?

What part of each day remains forever?

[POEM FOR CLASS DISCUSSION]

ANNABEL LEE

Edgar Allan Poe

It was many and many a year ago,
  In a kingdom by the sea,
That a maiden there lived whom you may know
  By the name of Annabel Lee;
And this maiden she lived with no other thought
  Than to love and be loved by me.

ANNABEL LEE

She was a child and I was a child,
   In this kingdom by the sea,
But we loved with a love that was more than love —
   I and my Annabel Lee —
With a love that the wingèd seraphs of heaven
   Coveted her and me.

And this was the reason that, long ago,
   In this kingdom by the sea,
A wind blew out of a cloud by night
   Chilling my Annabel Lee;
So that her highborn kinsmen came
   And bore her away from me,
To shut her up in a sepulcher
   In this kingdom by the sea.

The angels, not half so happy in heaven,
   Went envying her and me —
Yes! that was the reason (as all men know,
   In this kingdom by the sea)
That the wind came out of the cloud, chilling
   And killing my Annabel Lee.

But our love it was stronger by far than the love
   Of those who were older than we —
   Of many far wiser than we —

And neither the angels in heaven above,
   Nor the demons down under the sea,
Can ever dissever my soul from the soul
   Of the beautiful Annabel Lee.

For the moon never beams, without bringing me dreams
   Of the beautiful Annabel Lee,
And the stars never rise but I see the bright eyes
   Of the beautiful Annabel Lee;
And so, all the night-tide, I lie down by the side
Of my darling, my darling, my life and my bride,
   In the sepulcher there by the sea,
   In her tomb by the sounding sea.

"HARK, HARK! THE LARK"

William Shakespeare

Hark, hark! the lark at heaven's gate sings,
   And Phœbus 'gins arise,
His steeds to water at those springs
   On chaliced flowers that lies;
And winking Mary-buds begin
   To ope their golden eyes:
With every thing that pretty is,
   My lady sweet, arise:
     Arise, arise!

        "Cymbeline," Act II, Scene iii

In this beautiful morning song, why does the poet place the lark, rather than any other bird, at heaven's gate?

Phœbus is here poetically used for the sun. Why? Look up "Phœbus" in the encyclopedia.

Give other names for the sun.

What is the meaning of "'gins," and why is it used here?

Why is the word "chaliced" used?

What Shakespeare here calls "springs" is found glistening on the flowers at early morn. What do you call it?

What are the steeds of "Phœbus"?

What is the force of "winking" in reference to a flower?

What are the golden eyes of the "Mary-buds"?

What other pretty things does the morning bring?

NOTE. The Mary-bud is thought to be the English marsh marigold that is so abundant in April along the wet meadows.

◇ ◇ ◇

[POEM FOR CLASS DISCUSSION]

GOD'S PRESENCE IN NATURE

THOMAS MOORE

Thou art, O God, the life and light
    Of all this wondrous world we see;
Its glow by day, its smile by night,
    Are but reflections caught from Thee.
Where'er we turn, Thy glories shine,
And all things fair and bright are Thine!

When Day, with farewell beam, delays
    Among the opening clouds of Even,
And we can almost think we gaze
    Through golden vistas into Heaven —

GOD'S PRESENCE IN NATURE

Those hues, that make the Sun's decline
So soft, so radiant, Lord! are Thine.

When Night, with wings of starry gloom,
    O'ershadows all the earth and skies,
Like some dark beauteous bird, whose plume
    Is sparkling with unnumbered eyes —
That sacred gloom, those fires divine,
So grand, so countless, Lord! are Thine.

When youthful Spring around us breathes,
    Thy Spirit warms her fragrant sigh;
And every flower the Summer wreathes
    Is born beneath that kindling eye.
Where'er we turn, Thy glories shine,
And all things fair and bright are Thine.

"BLOW, BLOW"

William Shakespeare

Blow, blow, thou winter wind,
Thou art not so unkind
   As man's ingratitude;
Thy tooth is not so keen,
Because thou art not seen,
   Although thy breath be rude.

. . . .

Freeze, freeze, thou bitter sky,
That dost not bite so nigh
   As benefits forgot:
Though thou the waters warp,
Thy sting is not so sharp
   As friend remember'd not.

           "As You Like It," Act II, Scene vii

How blows the wind in winter?

Does the comparison of man's ingratitude to winter wind seem apt?

What sensation does the biting wind give?

What do you think of ungrateful children? How is their ingratitude shown?

A spiritual writer has said, "Ingratitude (to God) causes the fountains of grace to run dry." Explain this as best you can.

Does seeing the instrument of pain increase suffering?

Does the sky freeze? Then explain "Freeze, freeze, thou bitter sky."

"As benefits forgot" is another way of saying what?

What is the meaning of "the waters warp"? You would say, "the waters ..."

Have you ever been forgotten by one you thought your friend?

The biting cold does really sting. What do you think of the comparison drawn?

[POEM FOR CLASS DISCUSSION]

SEA FEVER[1]

JOHN MASEFIELD

I must go down to the seas again, to the lonely sea and the sky,
And all I ask is a tall ship and a star to steer her by;
And the wheel's kick and the wind's song and the white sail's shaking,
And a gray mist on the sea's face, and a gray dawn breaking.

[1] Reprinted from John Masefield's *Collected Poems*. By permission of The Macmillan Company, publishers.

SEA FEVER

I must go down to the seas again, for the call of the running tide
Is a wild call and a clear call that may not be denied;
And all I ask is a windy day with the white clouds flying,
And the flung spray and the blown spume, and the sea-gulls crying.

I must go down to the seas again, to the vagrant gypsy life,
To the gull's way and the whale's way where the wind's like a whetted knife;
And all I ask is a merry yarn from a laughing fellow rover,
And quiet sleep and a sweet dream when the long trick's over.

"HE PRAYETH BEST"

Samuel Taylor Coleridge

"He prayeth best, who loveth best
All things both great and small;
For the dear God who loveth us,
He made and loveth all."

◇ ◇ ◇

Is it true that "He prayeth best, who loveth best"?
Do you remember an instance in the Bible that illustrates this truth?
Does the Lord's Prayer contain the same lesson?

What promise did our Lord make to His Apostles as a reward for brotherly love?
What should this love of "All things both great and small" produce in us?
Does this love have any bearing on our treatment of birds and animals?
Has not God shown His love for the plants and animals by the beauty He has put in them?
How has He shown His love for us, His children?

From what long poem is this stanza taken?

[POEM FOR CLASS DISCUSSION]
ON THE LOSS OF THE *ROYAL GEORGE*

WILLIAM COWPER

Toll for the brave!
    The brave that are no more.
All sunk beneath the wave,
    Fast by their native shore!

Eight hundred of the brave,
    Whose courage well was tried,
Had made the vessel heel,
    And laid her on her side.

A land breeze shook the shrouds,
    And she was overset;
Down went the *Royal George*,
    With all her crew complete.

Toll for the brave!
    Brave Kempenfelt is gone;
His last sea fight is fought,
    His work of glory done.

It was not in the battle;
    No tempest gave the shock;
She sprang no fatal leak;
    She ran upon no rock.

His sword was in its sheath,
   His fingers held the pen,
When Kempenfelt went down
   With twice four hundred men.

Weigh the vessel up
   Once dreaded by our foes!
And mingle with our cup
   The tear that England owes.

Her timbers yet are sound,
   And she may float again
Full charged with England's thunder,
   And plough the distant main.

But Kempenfelt is gone,
   His victories are o'er;
And he and his eight hundred
   Shall plough the wave no more.

THE VIRGIN

William Wordsworth

Mother! whose virgin bosom was uncrost
With the least shade of thought to sin allied;
Woman! above all women glorified,
Our tainted nature's solitary boast;
Purer than foam on central Ocean tost;
Brighter than eastern skies at daybreak strewn
With fancied roses, than the unblemished moon
Before her wane begins on heaven's blue coast;
Thy Image falls to earth. Yet some, I ween,
Not unforgiven the suppliant knee might bend
As to a visible Power, in which did blend
All that was mixed and reconciled in Thee
Of mother's love with maiden purity,
Of high with low, celestial with terrene.

These lines were written by one who was not a Catholic, but who has paid high tribute to our Immaculate Mother. The fourth line is very frequently quoted.

What privilege of our Blessed Mother is extolled in the first two lines?

How was our Lady glorified above all women?
Why is she "Our tainted nature's solitary boast"?

How does the poet magnify Mary's purity and her brightness? Are not these comparisons beautiful and apt? Name some of the titles by which the Blessed Virgin is called in her Litany.

Why is the phrase "visible Power" used here?

What are the qualities "mixed and reconciled" in our Blessed Mother?

What is the meaning of "terrene"?

In this selection are there any words unfamiliar to you?

What other poems about our dear Mother do you know?

[POEM FOR CLASS DISCUSSION]

HYMN TO THE VIRGIN

Sir Walter Scott

Ave Maria! maiden mild!
   Listen to a maiden's prayer!
Thou canst hear though from the wild,
   Thou canst save amid despair.
Safe may we sleep beneath thy care,
   Though banished, outcast, and reviled —
Maiden! hear a maiden's prayer;
   Mother, hear a suppliant child!
                     Ave Maria!

HYMN TO THE VIRGIN

Ave Maria! undefiled!
  The flinty couch we now must share
Shall seem with down of eider piled,
  If thy protection hover there.
The murky cavern's heavy air
  Shall breathe of balm if thou hast smiled;
Then, Maiden! hear a maiden's prayer,
  Mother, list a suppliant child!
                    Ave Maria!

Ave Maria! stainless styled!
  Foul demons of the earth and air,
From this their wonted haunt exiled,
  Shall flee before thy presence fair.
We bow us to our lot of care,
  Beneath thy guidance reconciled:
Hear for a maid a maiden's prayer,
  And for a father hear a child!
                    Ave Maria!

APOSTROPHE TO THE OCEAN

Lord Byron

Roll on, thou deep and dark blue Ocean, roll!
Ten thousand fleets sweep over thee in vain;
Man marks the earth with ruin, his control
Stops with the shore; upon the watery plain
The wrecks are all thy deed, nor doth remain
A shadow of man's ravage save his own,
When, for a moment, like a drop of rain,
He sinks into thy depths with bubbling groan,
Without a grave, unknell'd, uncoffin'd, and unknown.

◇ ◇ ◇

Is the water of the ocean really blue?

"Ten thousand fleets" descending upon an army would demolish it. Have they any effect upon the power of the ocean?

How does man mark the earth with ruin?

Is it not true that man's "control Stops with the shore"? Who alone is master of the tempest and of the sea? How does Holy Scripture tell us that God set a limit to the waters?

How did God on various occasions show His dominion over the sea?

How has the ocean defied the power of man? Was not the sinking of the *Titanic* a rebuke to human skill and prowess? What other great sea disasters have you heard of?

To what is man compared when he sinks into a watery grave?

What is the meaning of "unknell'd"?

Of the four sorrows enumerated in the last line, which is greatest?

Find other poems relative to the "Ocean."

[POEM FOR CLASS DISCUSSION]

THE SEA

BARRY CORNWALL

The sea! the sea! the open sea!
The blue, the fresh, the ever free!
Without a mark, without a bound,
It runneth the earth's wide regions round;
It plays with the clouds, it mocks the skies;
Or like a cradled creature lies.

I'm on the sea! I'm on the sea!
I am where I would ever be;
With the blue above, and the blue below,
And silence wheresoe'er I go;
If a storm should come and awake the deep,
What matter? I shall ride and sleep.

I love, oh how I love to ride
On the fierce, foaming, bursting tide,
When every mad wave drowns the moon,
Or whistles aloft his tempest tune,
And tells how goeth the world below,
And why the southwest blasts do blow.

I never was on the dull, tame shore,
But I loved the great sea more and more,
And backward flew to her billowy breast,
Like a bird that seeketh its mother's nest;
And a mother she was, and is, to me;
For I was born on the open sea!

The waves were white, and red the morn,
In the noisy hour when I was born;
And the whale it whistled, the porpoise rolled,
And the dolphins bared their backs of gold;
And never was heard such an outcry wild
As welcomed to life the ocean child!

I've lived since then in calm and strife,
Full fifty summers a sailor's life,
With wealth to spend and a power to range,
But never have sought nor sighed for change;
And Death, whenever he comes to me,
Shall come on the wild, unbounded sea!

"MY HEART LEAPS UP WHEN I BEHOLD"

William Wordsworth

My heart leaps up when I behold
    A rainbow in the sky:
So was it when my life began;
So is it now I am a man;
So be it when I shall grow old,
    Or let me die!
The Child is father of the Man;
And I could wish my days to be
Bound each to each by natural piety.

What emotion do you experience when you see "A rainbow in the sky"? In what does its beauty consist?

When God placed the rainbow in the heavens, what promise did He make and to whom?

When and where would you look for a rainbow?

What is the old fable about the end of the rainbow? Did you ever believe it?

Bring to class all the poems you can find about the rainbow, and all those that contain the word.

What periods of life are named in this poem? Which two periods are most alike? How are they so? What application has this old proverb, "Once a man and twice a boy"?

What did our Blessed Lord say to His Apostles about spiritual childhood?

Explain the line "The Child is father of the Man." Is that a true statement?

The phrase "natural piety" carries out the relation between the child and the man. What virtues grow out of this "natural piety"? Are these the same as supernatural virtues? Can we have one without the other?

◇ ◇ ◇

[POEM FOR CLASS DISCUSSION]

"THE YEAR'S AT THE SPRING"

Robert Browning

The year's at the spring
And day's at the morn;
Morning's at seven;
The hillside's dew-pearl'd;
The lark's on the wing;
The snail's on the thorn:
God's in his heaven —
All's right with the world!

ON HIS BLINDNESS

John Milton

When I consider how my light is spent
Ere half my days, in this dark world and wide,
And that one talent which is death to hide
Lodged with me useless, though my soul more bent
To serve therewith my Maker, and present
My true account, lest He returning chide;
"Doth God exact day-labour, light denied?"
I fondly ask. But Patience, to prevent
That murmur, soon replies, "God doth not need
Either man's work or his own gifts. Who best
Bear his mild yoke, they serve him best. His state
Is kingly: thousands at his bidding speed,
And post o'er land and ocean without rest;
They also serve who only stand and wait."

   How old was Milton when he lost his sight?
   How does the poet tell us that he is blind?
   What word in the second line emphasizes the state of blindness?

What is the one talent of which he writes?

Why is it death to hide it? The "Parable of the Talents" answers this question. Relate the story.

Give the scriptural words of which Milton might have been thinking when he wrote, "present My True account, lest He returning chide."

Would you call the next line, the poet's question, a murmur? He speaks of it as such. Why?

Is not the answer of Patience most true?

Does God need either man's work or his own gifts? If you reply No, then why should any of us labor?

Does service necessarily imply a need?

How could you express this thought, "Who best Bear his mild yoke, they serve him best"? Christ said, "My meat is to do the will of Him who sent Me." Does this explain Milton's line?

Who are the thousands that at Christ's bidding speed o'er land and ocean without rest?

Who are they who also serve and wait?

Someone has said, "Prayer to Christ is good, work for Christ is better, and suffering with Christ best of all." Do you think the saying true? Are not prayer, work, and suffering inseparable links in the chain of true service?

[POEM FOR CLASS DISCUSSION]

"HOW SLEEP THE BRAVE"

William Collins

How sleep the brave, who sink to rest
By all their country's wishes blessed!
When Spring, with dewy fingers cold,
Returns to deck their hallowed mold,
She there shall dress a sweeter sod
Than Fancy's feet have ever trod.

By fairy hands their knell is rung,
By forms unseen their dirge is sung:
There Honor comes, a pilgrim gray,
To bless the turf that wraps their clay;
And Freedom shall awhile repair
To dwell a weeping hermit there!

THE RAIN SONG

Robert Loveman

It isn't raining rain to me,
   It's raining daffodils;
In every dimpled drop I see
   Wild flowers on the hills;
The clouds of gray engulf the day
   And overwhelm the town;
It isn't raining rain to me,
   It's raining roses down.

It isn't raining rain to me,
   But fields of clover bloom,
Where every buccaneering bee
   May find a bed and room;
A health unto the happy!
   A fig for him who frets!
It isn't raining rain to me,
   It's raining violets.

Does the poet mean just what he says in the first two lines? What do you think he means? Have you

THE RAIN SONG

ever seen the rain falling in "dimpled drop"? Name some of the wild flowers that the rain will bring. Do you remember the old proverb, "April showers bring forth May flowers"? Are the clouds gray? How do they "engulf" the day?

At what season are the fields covered with clover bloom? What is a buccaneer? How can "buccaneering" refer to a bee? What are his "bed and room"? Compare the next two lines with the corresponding lines in the first stanza. Do you think they carry out the thought as completely as do the lines

"The clouds of gray engulf the day
And overwhelm the town"?

Try to compose two lines of your own that will improve the second stanza. (Keep the word "frets" to rhyme with "violets." You may find its use as a noun more suitable.)

The thought in this little poem is worthy of being carried through life. So many of the little drab, dull things of life have a part in God's plan, as helpful and important to our well-being as rain is to spring flowers.

[POEM FOR CLASS DISCUSSION]

LOCHINVAR [1]

Sir Walter Scott

O, young Lochinvar is come out of the west;
Through all the wide border his steed was the best,
And save his good broadsword, he weapons had none;
He rode all unarmed, and he rode all alone.
So faithful in love, and so dauntless in war,
There never was knight like the young Lochinvar.

He stayed not for brake, and he stopped not for stone,
He swam the Eske River where ford there was none;
But ere he alighted at Netherby gate
The bride had consented, the gallant came late:
For a laggard in love, and a dastard in war
Was to wed the fair Ellen of brave Lochinvar.

So boldly he entered the Netherby Hall,
Among bridesmen, and kinsmen, and brothers, and
    all;
Then spoke the bride's father, his hand on his sword
(For the poor craven bridegroom said never a word),
"O, come ye in peace here, or come ye in war,
Or to dance at our bridal, young Lord Lochinvar?"

[1] From "Marmion."

"I long wooed your daughter, my suit you denied —
Love swells like the Solway, but ebbs like its tide, —
And now am I come, with this lost love of mine,
To lead but one measure, drink one cup of wine.
There are maidens in Scotland more lovely by far,
That would gladly be bride to the young Lochinvar."

The bride kissed the goblet, the knight took it up,
He quaffed off the wine, and he threw down the cup.
She looked down to blush, and she looked up to sigh,
With a smile on her lips, and a tear in her eye.
He took her soft hand, ere her mother could bar —
"Now tread we a measure!" said young Lochinvar.

So stately his form, and so lovely her face,
That never a hall such a galliard did grace,
While her mother did fret, and her father did fume,
And the bridegroom stood dangling his bonnet and plume;
And the bridemaidens whispered, "'Twere better by far
To have matched our fair cousin with young Lochinvar."

One touch to her hand, and one word in her ear,
When they reached the hall door, and the charger stood near;

So light to the croupe the fair lady he swung,
So light to the saddle before her he sprung!
"She is won! we are gone, over bank, bush, and scaur;
They'll have fleet steeds that follow," quoth young Lochinvar.

There was mounting 'mong Graemes of the Netherby clan;
Forsters, Fenwicks, and Musgraves, they rode and they ran:
There was racing and chasing on Cannobie Lea,
But the lost bride of Netherby ne'er did they see.
So daring in love, and so dauntless in war,
Have ye e'er heard of gallant like young Lochinvar?

HYMN TO THE SUN[1]

St. Francis of Assisi

Most high, omnipotent, good Lord,
Praise, glory and honor and benediction all, are Thine.
To Thee alone do they belong, Most High,
And there is no man fit to mention Thee.
Praise be to Thee, my Lord, with all Thy creatures,
Especially to my worshipful brother sun,
The which lights up the day, and through him dost Thou brightness give;
And beautiful is he and radiant with splendor great;
Of Thee, Most High, signification gives.
Praised be my Lord, for sister moon and for the stars,
In heaven Thou hast formed them clear and precious and fair.
Praised be my Lord for brother wind
And for the air and clouds and fair and every kind of weather,
By the which Thou givest to Thy creatures nourishment.

---

[1] Translated by Father Paschal Robinson, O. F. M.

Praised be my Lord for sister water,
The which is greatly helpful and humble and precious and pure.
Praised be my Lord for brother fire,
By the which Thou lightest up the dark.
And fair is he and gay and mighty and strong.
Praised be my Lord for our sister, mother earth,
The which sustains and keeps us
And brings forth diverse fruits with grass and flowers bright.
Praised be my Lord for those who for Thy love forgive
And weakness bear and tribulation.
Blessed those who shall in peace endure,
For by Thee, Most High, shall they be crowned.
Praised be my Lord for our sister, the bodily death,
From the which no living man can flee.
Woe to them who die in mortal sin;
Blessed those who shall find themselves in Thy most holy will,
For the second death shall do them no ill.
Praise ye and bless ye my Lord, and give Him thanks,
And be subject unto Him with great humility.

In this beautiful canticle, St. Francis teaches a model form of prayer. First he praises and blesses God for His

HYMN TO THE SUN

own most excellent attributes. Then he magnifies God for the mighty works of His creation.

Why does St. Francis call these various creatures "brothers" or "sisters"?

Enumerate those he designates as "brothers" and those he calls "sisters," and give the reason for this distinction.

What gifts are magnified in each of these creatures, and to whom is the glory thereof attributed?

What is frequently our attitude toward wind, weather, and fire? St. Francis habitually bore the frame of mind indicated here. What do you call this disposition?

Name the gifts the earth produces besides those St. Francis enumerates.

What virtues in man does St. Francis extol? Name other virtues that we should strive to acquire.

Do you think "death" worthy of being called our "sister"? Why?

Is there direct contrast between mortal sin and conformity to God's holy will? How does St. Francis express this truth?

What is meant by "the second death"?

[POEM FOR CLASS DISCUSSION]

HYMN[1]

St. Francis Xavier

My God, I love Thee, not because
    I hope for heaven thereby;
Nor because they who love Thee not
    Must burn eternally.

Thou, O my Jesus, Thou didst me
    Upon the cross embrace;
For me didst bear the nails and spear,
    And manifold disgrace;

And griefs and torments numberless;
    And sweat of agony;
E'en death itself, — and all for one
    Who was Thine enemy.

Then why, O blessèd Jesus Christ!
    Should I not love Thee well;
Not for the sake of winning heaven,
    Or of escaping hell:

[1] Translated from the Latin by Edward Caswell.

HYMN

Not with the hope of gaining aught;
   Not seeking a reward;
But as Thyself hast lovèd me,
   O, ever-loving Lord!

E'en so I love Thee, and will love
   And in thy praise will sing;
Solely because Thou art my God,
   And my eternal King!

THE VISION OF SIR LAUNFAL

James Russell Lowell

PRELUDE TO PART FIRST

And what is so rare as a day in June?
   Then, if ever, come perfect days;
Then Heaven tries earth if it be in tune,
   And over it softly her warm ear lays;
Whether we look, or whether we listen,
We hear life murmur, or see it glisten;
Every clod feels a stir of might,
   An instinct within it that reaches and towers,
And, groping blindly above it for light,
   Climbs to a soul in grass and flowers;
The flush of life may well be seen
   Thrilling back over hills and valleys;
The cowslip startles in meadows green,
   The buttercup catches the sun in its chalice,
And there's never a leaf nor a blade too mean
   To be some happy creature's palace;
The little bird sits at his door in the sun,
   Atilt like a blossom among the leaves,
And lets his illumined being o'errun
   With the deluge of summer it receives;

His mate feels the eggs beneath her wings,
And the heart in her dumb breast flutters and sings,
He sings to the wide world, and she to her nest, —
In the nice ear of Nature which song is the best?

◇ ◇ ◇

The description above is a beautiful picture of a perfect June day.

What is Heaven's "warm ear"?

What are some of the murmurs heard? Name some of the things that "glisten."

Does the line "Every clod feels a stir of might," mean that every clod is productive?

How do you know that the "instinct within it . . . reaches and towers"?

It is the soul in man that gives life and energy to his body. Does this fact justify the line "Climbs to a soul in grass and flowers"? Explain how it does so.

What are the indications of the "flush of life . . . over hills and valleys"?

Explain the line "The buttercup catches the sun in its chalice."

Are the two lines that follow clear to you? What have you seen that explains them?

What is the little bird's "door"?

To what is the reference "Atilt like a blossom among the leaves"?

What illumines his being?

Why is the word "deluge" used in the next line?
Which is the sweeter song, that which is sung to the whole world or the lullaby of motherhood?

[POEM FOR CLASS DISCUSSION]

THE VISION OF SIR LAUNFAL

JAMES RUSSELL LOWELL

PRELUDE TO PART SECOND

Down swept the chill wind from the mountain peak,
    From the snow five thousand summers old;
On open wold and hilltop bleak
    It had gathered all the cold,
And whirled it like sleet on the wanderer's cheek;
It carried a shiver everywhere
From the unleafed boughs and pastures bare;
The little brook heard it and built a roof
'Neath which he could house him, winter-proof;
All night by the white stars' frosty gleams
He groined his arches and matched his beams;
Slender and clear were his crystal spars
As the lashes of light that trim the stars;
He sculptured every summer delight
In his halls and chambers out of sight;

Sometimes his tinkling waters slipt
Down through a frost-leaved forest crypt,
Long, sparkling aisles of steel-stemmed trees
Bending to counterfeit a breeze;
Sometimes the roof no fretwork knew
But silvery mosses that downward grew;
Sometimes it was carved in sharp relief
With quaint arabesques of ice-fern leaf;
Sometimes it was simply smooth and clear
For the gladness of heaven to shine through, and here
He had caught the nodding bulrush-tops
And hung them thickly with diamond drops,
That crystalled the beams of moon and sun,
And made a star of every one:
No mortal builder's most rare device
Could match this winter-palace of ice;
'Twas as if every image that mirrored lay
In his depths serene through the summer day,
Each fleeting shadow of earth and sky,
   Lest the happy model should be lost,
Had been mimicked in fairy masonry
   By the elfin builders of the frost.

ODE TO A NIGHTINGALE

John Keats

Thou wast not born for death, immortal Bird!
   No hungry generations tread thee down;
The voice I hear this passing night was heard
   In ancient days by emperor and clown:
Perhaps the self-same song that found a path
     Through the sad heart of Ruth, when, sick for home,
She stood in tears amid the alien corn;
     The same that oft-times hath
   Charm'd magic casements, opening on the foam
Of perilous seas, in faery lands forlorn.

◇ ◇ ◇

You will, perhaps, not understand all the beauty of this stanza from the immortal ode of Keats; but if this brief study induces you to read all the poem, its end will be accomplished.

Notice that much of the poem is in the form of an address. This is a characteristic of the ode.

Critics have said that Keats reached the summit of lyric poetry in the lines

"Perhaps the self-same song that found a path
   Through the sad heart of Ruth, when, sick for home,
She stood in tears amid the alien corn."

Certainly there is exquisite tenderness in these lines that express universal emotion and yet make appeal to every human heart.

Love of home is a sacred fire that burns steadily and intensely in every heart, however dead to other emotions. This fire may flicker and burn low at times, but it can never be extinguished.

By the "immortal Bird" Keats meant lyric poetry, which will indeed never die because it is the language of emotions familiar to all. Hunger and thirst will never still this voice which sounds through royal halls and humble cottages. "The voice . . . heard . . . by emperor and clown" and the "self-same song that found a path through the sad heart of Ruth" were homesickness. Lyric poetry plays on the heartstring of many emotions, reaching out to romance and mystery, which Keats signified by "Charm'd magic casements, opening on the foam."

[POEM FOR CLASS DISCUSSION]

RUTH

Thomas Hood

She stood breast-high amid the corn,
Clasped by the golden light of morn,
Like the sweetheart of the sun,
Who many a glowing kiss had won.

On her cheek an autumn flush,
Deeply ripen'd; — such a blush
In the midst of brown was born,
Like red poppies grown with corn.

Round her eyes her tresses fell,
Which were blackest none could tell,
But long lashes veiled a light,
That had else been all too bright.

And her hat, with shady brim,
Made her tressy forehead dim; —
Thus she stood amid the stooks,
Praising God with sweetest looks.

Sure, I said, Heav'n did not mean,
Where I reap thou should'st but glean;
Lay thy sheaf adown and come,
Share my harvest and my home.

BIOGRAPHICAL INDEX

BELLOC, HILAIRE, an English Catholic historian, publicist, and poet, was born in 1870, and was educated at Balliol College, Oxford. He has been a soldier, a journalist, and a member of the British Parliament. He is the author of many books.

BLAKE, WILLIAM (1757-1827), was born in London of poor parents, who could afford to give him but little schooling. He early evinced great talent for painting and for writing. His pictures were worthy of a place in the Royal Academy. *Poetical Sketches*, *Songs of Experience*, and *Songs of Innocence* are among his best works.

BLUNT, HUGH FRANCIS, Catholic poet-priest, was born at Medway, Massachusetts, in 1877, and was educated at Boston College, and at St. John's Seminary, where he received Holy Orders. He is the author of many books in prose and in poetry. *Poems, Songs for Sinners, The Book of the Mother of God*, and *Spiritual Songs* are among his best-known publications.

BROWNING, ELIZABETH BARRETT (1806-1861), was born at Durham, England. She received a liberal education and was a noted classical scholar. She became the wife of Robert Browning, the celebrated English poet.

BROWNING, ROBERT (1812-1889), an English poet of high rank, was born in a suburb of London. His father carefully supervised his early years of study. After graduation from University College, London, he went to Italy to study medieval history and Italian culture. Browning's greatest poem is "The Ring and the Book."

BIOGRAPHICAL INDEX

BRYANT, WILLIAM CULLEN (1794-1878), an American poet and journalist, was born at Cummington, Massachusetts. "Thanatopsis," his most widely known poem, was composed when Bryant was but eighteen years of age.

BURNS, ROBERT (1759-1796), a Scottish poet of rare merit, was born at Alloway, near Ayr. He received only a grammar-school education. Most of his education was acquired from extensive and intensive reading.

BYRON, GEORGE GORDON, LORD (1788-1824), an English poet and peer, was born in London. He spent two years in Trinity College. He had natural genius and poetic instinct, and in his short life wrote many remarkable poems. His death is the greatest of his works, for he died fighting for the liberty of Greece.

CAMPBELL, THOMAS (1777-1844), was born in Glasgow, Scotland. He was educated in the university of his native city. His lyrics are his finest productions.

CARLIN, FRANCIS (J. F. C. MACDONNELL), was born at Bay Shore, Long Island, in 1881. He now resides in New York City and is engaged entirely in creative literary work. His two books of poems, *My Ireland* and *A Cairn of Stars*, have won him high praise from critics here and elsewhere.

CARLYLE, THOMAS (1795-1881), an English biographer, essayist, and historian, was born in Scotland and was educated at Edinburgh University. His whole life was devoted to literary work.

COLERIDGE, SAMUEL TAYLOR (1772-1834), was born at Ottery St. Mary's, Devonshire, England. He was educated at Christ's Hospital, and at Cambridge, where he received the prize for writing the best Greek ode. His finest poem is "The Rime of the Ancient Mariner."

BIOGRAPHICAL INDEX

COLLINS, WILLIAM (1721-1759), an English poet, was born at Chichester and was educated at Oxford. His odes rank high among the lyrics of our language.

CORNWALL, BARRY (1787-1874), was the pen name of Bryan Waller Procter. His daughter, Adelaide Anne, is better known to Catholics because of her conversion to the Church in 1850. She wrote many poems which are deeply Catholic in spirit.

COWPER, WILLIAM (1731-1800), an English poet, was born in Hertfordshire, and received his education in private schools and at Westminster. He was nearly fifty-five years of age before he was given any recognition as a writer.

CRASHAW, RICHARD (1613?-1649), was born in London. He was educated at Cambridge and attained a high place in scholarship. He became a Catholic in 1646, and his writings bear witness to the integrity of his faith. His poems are largely religious lyrics.

DALY, THOMAS AUGUSTINE, a Catholic poet, was born in Philadelphia in 1871. He was educated at Villanova College and at Fordham University. He is prominent as an author and journalist. His best-known, though not his best, poems are in the dialects of the Irish and Italian immigrants.

DONNELLY, ELEANOR C. (1848-1917), a Catholic American poetess, was born in Philadelphia. From her early years she wrote poetry. Her "Vision of the Monk Gabriel" was written eight years before Longfellow's "Legend Beautiful" appeared. Both poems are based on the same legend.

EDEN, HELEN PARRY, a daughter of Judge Parry, was born in 1885. She was educated at Manchester University. With her husband, Denis Eden, the artist, she was received into the Catholic Church in 1909. She is the author of *A String of Sapphires*, a rhymed life of our Lord for children.

BIOGRAPHICAL INDEX

EMERSON, RALPH WALDO (1803–1882), an American poet, was born in Boston and was educated at Harvard University. He was ordained a minister of the Unitarian Church, but resigned his pastorate because he could not agree with the views of his congregation. His poetry possesses rare beauty of expression.

FEENEY, LEONARD, S. J., was born at Lynn, Massachusetts, in 1897. He entered the Society of Jesus in 1914, and was ordained priest in 1928. He is the author of *In Towns and Little Towns*, a charming collection of verse.

FIELD, EUGENE (1850–1895), an American poet, was born in St. Louis, Missouri. He studied at Williams and Knox colleges and at the University of Missouri, but without taking a degree. He was a "newspaper poet," and most of his poems appeared in the *Denver Tribune* or the *Chicago Daily News*.

FRANCIS OF ASSISI, ST. (1181–1226), was born at Assisi, Umbria, Italy, the son of a wealthy cloth merchant. He received his education from the priests of St. George in Assisi and devoted himself to the gay life of a troubadour. Later he turned his talents to God, founded the Franciscan Order, and became truly the "Troubadour of God." He has been called the precursor of Dante.

FRANCIS XAVIER, ST. (1506–1552), was born in the castle of Xavier, near Navarre, Spain. He studied at the Collége de Sainte-Barbe, in Paris, where he met St. Ignatius Loyola. He was ordained with Ignatius in 1537. He labored with great success in Japan and India. When he was en route to China, he died on an island off the Chinese coast.

HERRICK, ROBERT (1591–1674), was born at Cheapside, London. He was educated at St. John's College and at

Trinity Hall, Cambridge. He wrote more than a thousand poems, some of which are very fine lyrics.

HODGSON, RALPH, was born in Yorkshire in 1872. For a time he lived in America. He has worked successively as pressman, draftsman, and editor. He is the author of *The Last Blackbird* and *Poems*.

HOOD, THOMAS (1799–1845), an English poet and humorist, was born in London. He began his literary career early in life. "The Song of the Shirt" and "The Bridge of Sighs" are his best-known poems.

HUNT, LEIGH (1784–1859), an English poet and essayist, was born at Southgate, near London. "The Story of Rimini" is considered his best poem.

INGELOW, JEAN (1820–1897), an English poetess and novelist, was born at Boston, Lincolnshire. Among her poems is a ballad, "The High Tide on the Coast of Lincolnshire."

KEATS, JOHN (1795–1821), a great English poet, was born in London. His circumstances did not permit a university education. He died at a very early age, leaving to posterity some of the finest odes in English literature.

KELLY, BLANCHE MARY, was born at Troy, New York, in 1881, and was educated at the Convent of the Sacred Heart, Albany. She was for several years a member of the editorial board of *The Catholic Encyclopedia*. She is now a member of the teaching staff at Mount St. Vincent's College.

KILMER, JOYCE (1886–1918), poet and literary critic, was born in New Brunswick, New Jersey. He was educated at Rutgers College and at Columbia University. After teaching for a short time he became a journalist. His conversion to the Catholic Church took place in 1913. He enlisted in the

World War and was killed in battle. His most popular poem is "Trees," which has been put to music.

LANIER, SIDNEY (1842–1881), an American poet, was born at Macon, Georgia, and was graduated with honor from Oglethorpe College. He served in the Confederate Army, practiced law, wrote poetry, and lectured at the Johns Hopkins University. "Corn" and "The Song of the Chattahoochee" are among his best poems.

LONGFELLOW, HENRY WADSWORTH (1807–1882), our best-loved American poet, was born in Portland, Maine. He was educated at Bowdoin College. He taught for six years at his Alma Mater and for nearly twenty years at Harvard. Longfellow's poems are known and loved in both hemispheres.

LOVEMAN, ROBERT (1864–1923), was born at Cleveland, Ohio. He received his education in Dalton, Georgia, and in the University of Alabama. He traveled extensively and studied abroad. He is the author of *A Book of Silence*, *Songs from a Georgia Garden*, *On the Way to Millowdale*, and *Sonnets of the Strife*.

LOWELL, JAMES RUSSELL (1819–1891), an American poet and diplomat, was born in Boston, Massachusetts, and was educated at Harvard University. His best-known poem is "The Vision of Sir Launfal."

MCCARTHY, DENIS A., a journalist, poet, and lecturer, was born in Carrick-on-Suir, County Tipperary, Ireland, July 25, 1870. His first schooling was received from the Christian Brothers of his native town. He came to the United States at fifteen years of age. He is the author of several books of Irish ballads and patriotic American poems. He is on the editorial staff of Ginn and Company.

MCCRAE, JOHN D. (1872–1918), born in Scotland, was early taken to Canada, where he remained until the outbreak of the World War. "In Flanders Fields" was written during the war, in which he served, and he died a lieutenant in the Medical Corps.

MASEFIELD, JOHN, was born in Shropshire, England, in 1878. In his boyhood he followed a seafaring life. He came to America, almost destitute. While employed in a restaurant in Yonkers he purchased a volume of Chaucer's poems. The reading of these poems was the beginning of his poetic aspirations.

MEYNELL, ALICE (1850–1922), an English writer of verse, was the wife of Wilfred Meynell, the critic. She and her sister, Lady Butler, the painter, were carefully educated by their father. "The Shepherdess" is Mrs. Meynell's most frequently quoted poem.

MILLER, JOAQUIN (1841–1913), was the pen name of Cincinnatus Heine Miller, who was born in Indiana. He was a man of many different avocations and was, in turn, miner, lawyer, journalist, fruit grower, and soldier. His *Songs of the Sierras* gave him recognition as a poet.

MILTON, JOHN (1608–1674), a great English poet, was born in London. He took his degrees at Cambridge. Constant study affected his eyes, and he became totally blind twenty years before his death. Milton's greatest work is "Paradise Lost."

MOORE, THOMAS (1779–1852), who has been called "Ireland's national poet," was born in Dublin and was educated at Trinity College in his native city. His reputation as a poet rests principally upon his *Irish Melodies*.

MORLEY, CHRISTOPHER, was born at Haverford, Pennsylvania, in 1890. After his graduation from Haverford College he went as a Rhodes Scholar to New College, Oxford. He has been engaged in literary work since 1913.

NEWMAN, JOHN HENRY, CARDINAL (1801-1890), was born in London and was educated at Ealing, and at Trinity College, Oxford, where he was graduated with classical honors. He was ordained in the Anglican Church, but made his abjuration and entered the Catholic Church in 1845. He was a priest, head of the Oratory of St. Philip Neri, and afterwards was rector of the Catholic University of Dublin. He was created a cardinal in 1879. He produced some remarkable literary works, and it has been said of his style that it is as near perfection as prose has ever been.

PATMORE, COVENTRY (1823-1896), a Catholic poet, was born at Woodford, Essex, England. He became assistant librarian at the British Museum in 1846. His finest poem is "The Angel of the House."

PLUNKETT, JOSEPH M. (1887-1916), son of Count Plunkett, was born at Dublin. He was educated at Stonyhurst, England. He planned the Easter Rising in 1916, and, upon the suppression of the revolt, he was condemned to death by the British authorities.

POE, EDGAR ALLAN (1809-1849), an American poet of rare genius, was born in Boston. At an early age he was adopted by a wealthy merchant of Richmond. He studied in England for some years, then for a short time at the University of Virginia. Later he attended West Point, from which he was expelled. Poe's literary career was marked by poverty, suffering, and disappointment. His most famous poem is "The Raven."

ROLLE, RICHARD (1290-1349), English hermit and author, was born near Pickering, Yorkshire. He was educated at Oxford. At the age of nineteen he left home to become a recluse. He wrote many poems and treatises of a high literary and spiritual order.

BIOGRAPHICAL INDEX

ROSSETTI, CHRISTINA G. (1830–1894), the sister of the poet and painter, Dante Gabriel Rossetti, was born in London and was educated under the direction of her mother, a woman of great refinement and culture. Her poems have been collected in several volumes.

RYAN, ABRAM J. (1839–1886), Catholic priest-poet, was born at Hagerstown, Maryland. He served as chaplain in the Confederate Army throughout the Civil War. "The Conquered Banner" is perhaps his finest poem.

SCOTT, SIR WALTER (1771–1832), a Scotch novelist and poet, was born in Edinburgh. He was educated at the high school and university of his native city and afterwards studied law. Among his romantic narrative poems are "The Lay of the Last Minstrel" and "The Lady of the Lake." *Ivanhoe* is the best of his novels.

SHAKESPEARE, WILLIAM (1564–1616), born at Stratford-on-Avon, England, is the greatest of all dramatists. Very little is known of his life. He received a grammar-school education and spent most of his life in London, writing plays and acting occasionally. He died at Stratford-on-Avon.

STEVENSON, ROBERT LOUIS (1850–1894), was born in Edinburgh, Scotland. He was educated in private schools and in the University of Edinburgh. He belonged to a family of celebrated engineers and his father wished him to continue in the family tradition, but Stevenson preferred a literary career. He wrote books of travel and fiction and *A Child's Garden of Verses*.

STODDARD, CHARLES WARREN (1843–1909), was born in Rochester, New York. He taught at Notre Dame, and at the Catholic University, Washington. His best work is *South Sea Idyls*.

TABB, JOHN BANNISTER (1845–1909), a convert to Catholicity, a priest, and a poet of rare skill, was born near Richmond, Virginia. He taught for years at St. Charles College, Baltimore. His poems have been collected in several volumes.

TEASDALE, SARA, was born at St. Louis, Missouri, in 1884. She was educated in the private schools of that city. She is the author of *Helen of Troy and Other Poems.*

TENNYSON, ALFRED (1809–1892), an English poet, was born in Lincolnshire, England. He was educated at Louth grammar school and at Cambridge University. He succeeded Wordsworth as poet laureate. *The Idylls of the King* gave him his place in literature.

THOMPSON, FRANCIS (1859–1907), a great Catholic poet, was born in Ashton, England, and was educated at Ushaw College. He studied medicine, but preferred to give his time to literature. His life was passed in poverty, and in dreams which were realized in great poetry. He was befriended by Alice Meynell and her husband. His best poem is "The Hound of Heaven."

TYNAN, KATHARINE (Mrs. Katharine Tynan Hinkson), was born at Clondalkin, near Dublin, in 1861. She has been for years a prolific writer of fiction and poetry, and has published several books of information and charming memoirs.

VAN DYKE, HENRY, an American educator and writer, was born in Germantown, Pennsylvania, in 1852. He was graduated from Princeton University and from the Presbyterian Seminary. He wrote *The Builders and Other Poems.*

WOLFE, CHARLES (1791–1823), an Irish Protestant clergyman and poet, was born at Dublin and was educated in his native city. "The Burial of Sir John Moore" is his best poem.

WORDSWORTH, WILLIAM (1770–1850), a celebrated English poet, was born in Cockermouth, Cumberland. He received a degree from St. John's College, Cambridge, and from Oxford. He succeeded Southey as poet laureate.

INDEX OF AUTHORS

ANONYMOUS   PAGE
    Before Sleeping 22
    Old Christmas Carol, An 58
    In the Fields 37

BELLOC, HILAIRE
    Courtesy 70

BIBLE, THE HOLY
    Magnificat, The 56
    Jubilate Deo 79

BLAKE, WILLIAM
    Lamb, The 23
    Tiger, The 24

BLUNT, HUGH F.
    Old Woman's Rosary, An 61

BROWNING, ELIZABETH BARRETT
    Child's Thought of God, A 26

BROWNING, ROBERT
    "Year's at the Spring, The" 122

BRYANT, WILLIAM CULLEN
    To the Fringed Gentian 45

INDEX OF AUTHORS

BURNS, ROBERT   PAGE
    Charity 72

BYRON, GEORGE GORDON, LORD
    Apostrophe to the Ocean 118

CAMPBELL, THOMAS
    Hohenlinden 86

CARLIN, FRANCIS
    Irish, The 38

CARLYLE, THOMAS
    To-day 80

COLERIDGE, SAMUEL TAYLOR
    Epitaph 33
    "He Prayeth Best" 112

COLLINS, WILLIAM
    "How Sleep the Brave" 125

CORNWALL, BARRY
    Sea, The 119

COWPER, WILLIAM
    On the Loss of the *Royal George* 113

CRASHAW, RICHARD
    Two Went Up to the Temple to Pray 7

DALY, THOMAS AUGUSTINE
    Da Leetla Boy 99

INDEX OF AUTHORS

DONNELLY, ELEANOR C.   PAGE
    Mary Immaculate 52

EDEN, HELEN PARRY
    Confessional, The 75

EMERSON, RALPH WALDO
    Rhodora, The 88

FEENEY, LEONARD, S.J.
    Way of the Cross, The 78

FIELD, EUGENE
    Little Boy Blue 97
    Wynken, Blynken, and Nod 17

FRANCIS OF ASSISI, ST.
    Hymn to the Sun 131

FRANCIS XAVIER, ST.
    Hymn 134

HERRICK, ROBERT
    To Daffodils 12

HODGSON, RALPH
    "Time, You Old Gipsy Man" 41

HOOD, THOMAS
    Ruth 142

HUNT, LEIGH
    Abou Ben Adhem 73
    Glove and the Lions, The 20

INDEX OF AUTHORS

INGELOW, JEAN   PAGE
    Seven Times One 31

KEATS, JOHN
    Ode to a Nightingale 140

KELLY, BLANCHE MARY
    Housewife's Prayer, The 96

KILMER, JOYCE
    Trees 4

LANIER, SIDNEY
    Ballad of Trees and the Master, A 34

LONGFELLOW, HENRY WADSWORTH
    Builders, The 15
    Day is Done, The 63

LOVEMAN, ROBERT
    Rain Song, The 126

LOWELL, JAMES RUSSELL
    Vision of Sir Launfal, The (Prelude to Part First) . . . 136
    Vision of Sir Launfal, The (Prelude to Part Second) . . 138

MCCARTHY, DENIS A.
    Green o' the Spring, The 47

MCCRAE, JOHN D.
    In Flanders Fields 84

MASEFIELD, JOHN
    Sea Fever 109

INDEX OF AUTHORS

MEYNELL, ALICE   PAGE
Shepherdess, The 94

MILLER, JOAQUIN
For those who Fail 53

MILTON, JOHN
On his Blindness 123

MOORE, THOMAS
God's Presence in Nature 106

MORLEY, CHRISTOPHER
Song for a Little House 27

NEWMAN, JOHN HENRY, CARDINAL
Song of the Angel 91

PATMORE, COVENTRY
Toys, The 29

PLUNKETT, JOSEPH M.
I see His Blood upon the Rose 36

POE, EDGAR ALLAN
Annabel Lee 102

ROLLE, RICHARD
"What is in Heaven?" 54

ROSSETTI, CHRISTINA G.
Green Cornfield, A 11

INDEX OF AUTHORS

RYAN, ABRAM J.   PAGE
    Child's Wish, A 59

SCOTT, SIR WALTER
    Hymn to the Virgin 116
    Lochinvar 128

SHAKESPEARE, WILLIAM
    "Blow, Blow" 108
    "Hark, Hark! the Lark" 105
    Justice 74
    Quality of Mercy, The 68

STEVENSON, ROBERT LOUIS
    Swing, The 40

STODDARD, CHARLES WARREN
    Ave Maria Bells 93

TABB, JONN BANNISTER
    Bunch of Roses, A 83
    Father Damien 82
    I Walked a Mile 67
    Tax-Gatherer, The 83
    Out of Bounds 77

TEASDALE, SARA
    Coin, The 5

TENNYSON, ALFRED
    "Break, Break, Break" 101
    Sweet and Low 66

INDEX OF AUTHORS

THOMPSON, FRANCIS   PAGE
    Little Jesus 1

TYNAN, KATHARINE
    Man of the House, The 49

VAN DYKE, HENRY
    Four Things 6

WOLFE CHARLES
    Burial of Sir John Moore, The 89

WORDSWORTH, WILLIAM
    "I Wandered Lonely as a Cloud" 8
    "My Heart leaps up when I Behold" 121
    Virgin, The 115

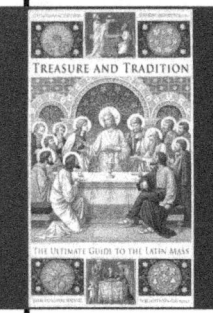

St. Augustine Academy Press

...because what children read really matters...

At St. Augustine Academy Press, we are dedicated to bringing you only solid Catholic literature from yesterday and today. To learn more, visit us online at

www.staapress.com

www.ingramcontent.com/pod-product-compliance
Lightning Source LLC
Chambersburg PA
CBHW031642040426
42453CB00006B/188